ACCESS 7

Moira Stephen

TEACH YOURSELF BOOKS

ISBN 0 340 69750-4

First published 1997
Impression number 10 9 8 7 6 5 4 3 2
Year   2000

Typeset by MacDesign, Southampton, Hampshire
Printed in Great Britain for Hodder & Stoughton Educational, a division of
Hodder Headline plc, 338 Euston Road, London NW1 3BH by Cox & Wyman Ltd,
Reading, Berkshire

——— CONTENTS ———

PREFACE

This book is for the user who wants to be able to harness the power of Access 7 *without* being overpowered by database jargon and difficult concepts. Whether you've never used a database in your life, or are familiar with databases but new to Access 7, this book will have you quickly up and running on this very popular package.

By using examples that are familiar to us all, this book takes you through the main processes that will help you build and use efficient Access 7 databases. You can either work from beginning to end (recommended for new users) or dip into any chapter that interests you and apply the techniques to your own database.

- **Database design**: What do you want from your database? What data will you need to store? How can you organise your data efficiently in a database? These areas are explored to help you develop and design your databases.

- **Jargon and concepts**: Jargon and new concepts are explained in layman's terms – you won't be bombarded with computer-speak!

- **Essential database skills**: Setting up table structures, entering and editing data and extracting data from your database are all explored in this book.

- **Ease of use**: Whether you are designing a database for your own use, or one for others to use, the interface between you and the data is very important. You will find out how to design friendly 'front-ends' for your databases, so that once a database is set up, it is easy to use.

- **Efficient working practices**: Finally, **macros** are introduced to give you an insight into how they can help you become more efficient as you use Access 7.

This book will be a useful teaching and learning aid, whether you are working by yourself or teaching others in a classroom situation. The fact that the book contains a main project that can be worked through makes it ideal teaching material.

I hope you enjoy Teach Yourself Access 7, and have success in working with your databases.

Moira Stephen

April 1997

1

GETTING STARTED

1.1 Aims of this chapter

This chapter introduces you to the Access 7 relational database management system (RDBMS). It explains the concept of an RDBMS and de-mystifies some jargon that might be new to you. It also gives an overview of the system requirements and installation procedure for the product. Finally, and very importantly, it highlights the need to plan and prepare your data, to help ensure that you get maximum benefit from using Access.

1.2 What is a database?

A database is simply a collection of data. For example, it may be your Christmas card name and address list, or details about books, CDs and videos in your library or it may be company data (with details of customers, suppliers, products sold, orders, employees). The data is *collected* and *organised* for a particular purpose.

Most modern database management systems (including Access) use the *relational* database management model. This simply means that all the data stored in the database is related to one subject, e.g. your company, or the items in your library.

In a simple database, it may be feasible to store all the information together in one table (see section 1.3 for a definition if necessary) – for instance, a Christmas card name and address list. Other databases are more complex – your library or company database for example. The data would then need to be divided up into several tables, which could be linked as and when required. Data about two classes of information (such as 'books' and 'publishers' in a library situation) can be manipulated as a single entry based on related data values.

For example, in your library you might want to store specific details on each book – title, author, category, ISBN, number held, year published, publisher, etc – on your system. It would be very repetitive (and pointless) to store all the name, address and other contact details for the publisher with each book detail, since you may have the same detail duplicated hundreds of times, if one publisher is responsible for many of your books.

Therefore, in a relational system, when you store information about a book, you include a data field that can be used to connect each book with its publisher details, e.g. *Publisher Code*. The publisher details would then be stored in a separate table. The name, address and contact details of each publisher would only need to be recorded once, and could be linked to any book through the *Publisher Code* field whenever necessary.

—————— 1.3 Database jargon ——————

Some database terminology may be unfamiliar to you. Below you will find brief definitions of the terms you are likely to encounter in the near future. Don't worry about trying to understand them all at once – things become clearer as you use Access.

Table

In a relational database, all the data on one topic is stored in a *table*. If your database requirements are fairly simple, you might have only one table in your database. If your requirements are more complex, your database may contain several tables. In the Library database example, you could have a table for your book data, one for your publisher data and perhaps one for author data.

The data in the table is structured in a way that will allow you to interrogate the data when and as required. All of the data on one item, e.g. a book or a publisher, is held in the *record* for that book or publisher, within the appropriate table.

Record

A *record* contains information about a single item in your table. All the detail relating to one book will be held in that book's record in the Book table. Information about a publisher will be held in a record for that publisher in the Publisher table. The record is broken down into several *fields* – one for each piece of detail about your item (book, publisher, etc.).

Field

A *field* is a piece of data within a record. In your book's record, things like book title, author-firstname, author-surname, category, number held, library code, location, ISBN, publisher code, etc. would all be held in separate fields. In a publisher record, you would have fields for name, address (perhaps separate fields for street, town, postcode, county), telephone number, fax number, e-mail address. etc.

Each field has a name that identifies it.

Relationship

This determines the way in which the detail in one table is related to the detail in another table, e.g. through the publisher code. Publishers would have a *one-to-many* relationship with books as one publisher could have published many books.

Join

The process of linking tables or queries.

Data definition

The process of defining what data will be stored in your database, specifying the data field's type (it might be numbers or characters), the data field's size and indicating how it is related to data in other tables.

Data manipulation

Once your data is set up, you can work with it in many ways – this may involve sorting it into a specific order, extracting specific records from tables, or listing detail from a number of different tables into one report.

———— 1.4 Schematic diagram ————

The diagram below illustrates a simple database. The *Book* table would be related to the *Publisher* table through the publisher code field. The *Book* table has been expanded to indicate what fields might be included in it. In the example, the *Author* table could be related to both the *Publisher* table and the *Book* table.

● Each ***record*** in a table is presented in a ***row*** – in this example each book is a record.
● Each ***field*** in a record is in a ***column*** – there is a *Title* field, *Author* field etc.
● Each field has a ***field name*** at the top of the column – *Title*, *Author*, *Category*.

Example of a Library Database

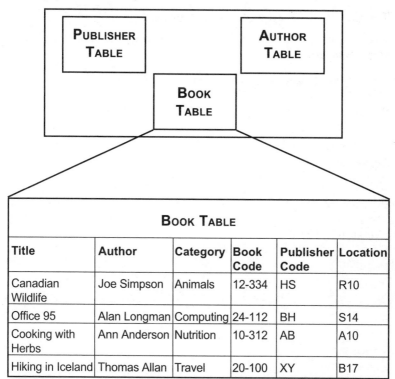

BOOK TABLE					
Title	Author	Category	Book Code	Publisher Code	Location
Canadian Wildlife	Joe Simpson	Animals	12-334	HS	R10
Office 95	Alan Longman	Computing	24-112	BH	S14
Cooking with Herbs	Ann Anderson	Nutrition	10-312	AB	A10
Hiking in Iceland	Thomas Allan	Travel	20-100	XY	B17

1.5 Access Objects

An Access database consists of *objects* that can be used to input, display, interrogate, print and automate your work. These Objects are listed in the **Database** window. The purpose of each object is summarised below.

Tables　　[▦ Tables]

Tables are the most important objects in your database. Tables are used for data entry and edit.

In a table, each record is displayed as a row and each field is displayed as a column. You can display a number of records on the screen at any one time, and as many fields as will fit on your screen. Any records or fields not displayed can be scrolled into view as required.

Queries ▣ Queries

You use Queries to locate specific records within your Tables. You might want to extract records that meet specific selection criteria (e.g. all employees on Grade G in the accounts department). When you run a Query, the results are arranged in columns and rows like a Table.

Forms ▣ Forms

You can use Forms to provide an alternative to tables for data entry and viewing records. With Forms, you arrange the fields as required on the screen – you can design your forms to look like the printed forms (invoices, order forms, etc.) that you use.

When you use Forms, you display one record at a time on your screen.

Reports ▣ Reports

Reports can be used to produce various printed outputs from data in your database. Using Reports, the same database can produce, for instance, a list of one publisher's books, a set of mailing labels for your letters, or a report on books in a specific category.

Macros & Modules ▣ Macros ▣ Modules

Macros and Modules are used to automate the way you use Access, and can be used to build some very sophisticated applications.

They are introduced at the end of this book.

1.6 System Requirements

To run Access 7 successfully on your computer, it should meet the following minimum hardware and software specifications. The first set gives the system requirements for Access 7 only, the second set gives details of additional requirements should you be installing all of the Microsoft Office Professional suite.

Specification for Access 7

Personal computer	386 DX or higher (486 recommended)
Operating system	Windows 95 or Windows NT (version 3.51 or later). NB Access 7 will not run on machines using earlier versions of Windows.
RAM	The more the better! ◆ 12 Mb if you're using Windows 95. ◆ 16 Mb if you're using Windows NT.
Hard disk	Depending on the amount of disk space you have available, you can choose from three different types of installation. ◆ **Compact** = 14 Mb ◆ **Typical** = 32 Mb ◆ **Custom** = 42 Mb (maximum)
Disk drive	One 3.5" high density disk drive (if you've bought the diskette version).
CD-ROM Drive	Optional but recommended – it's a lot quicker to set up your software using a CD rather than spend your day swapping lots of disks.
Monitor	VGA or higher resolution video adaptor (SVGA 256 colour recommended).
Mouse	Microsoft mouse, or compatible pointing device.
Printer	Any Windows compatible printer.

If you are installing the whole of the Microsoft Office Professional suite, the above specification applies, with the following amendments.

Specification for Microsoft Office Professional

RAM	◆ 12 Mb if you're using Windows 95 ◆ 16 Mb if you're using Windows NT These figures are required to run Access successfully, or to run any other two programs simultaneously (e.g. Word and Excel). If you think you'll run more than two programs at the same time, or a second program at the same time as Access, it's recommended that you have more RAM. At the time or writing (Spring 1997), memory is relatively cheap, so it's as good a time as any to add more to your machine!
Hard disk	Depending on the amount of disk space you have available, you can choose from three different types of installation. ◆ **Compact** = 40 Mb ◆ **Typical** = 87 Mb ◆ **Custom** = 126 Mb (maximum)

—————— 1.7 Installing Access ——————

If you have bought a new computer at the same time as purchasing your software, the software is most probably pre-installed on your hard disk. If this is the case you can skip this bit.

As the general trend is towards buying Office Suites (rather than individual applications) you have probably purchased Microsoft Office Professional (with Word, Excel, PowerPoint and all the other goodies that are thrown in).

The instructions below are for installing Microsoft Office Professional under Windows 95 or Windows NT – if you have bought Access on its own follow the instructions included with your CD or disk set.

Windows 95 version

1. If you're installing from a CD, insert the Office Professional CD in the CD-ROM drive on your computer

   If you're installing from floppy disks, insert the first Setup disk (Disk 1) in drive A or B

2. Click the **Start** button on the **Taskbar**

3. Choose **Settings**

4. Click **Control Panel**

5. Double click the **Add/Remove Programs** icon

6. On the **Install/Uninstall** tab, click the **Install...** button

7. Follow the **Set up** instructions on the screen

Windows NT version

1. If you're installing from a CD, insert the Office Professional CD in the CD-ROM drive on your computer

   If you're installing from floppy disks, insert the first Setup disk (Disk 1) in drive A or B

2. In **Program Manager**, click **Run** in the **File** menu

3. Enter the drive location you are installing from, followed by the word setup, e.g. if you are installing from drive A, type:

   a:\setup

4. Click **OK**

5. Follow the **Set up** instructions on the screen

───── 1.8 Preparing your data ─────

The most important (and often difficult) stage in setting up any database takes place away from the computer. Before you set up a database you must get your data organised.

There are two key questions that need to be addressed:

● What do I want to store?

● What information do I want to get out of my database?

Take your time and work out your answers before you start!

Once you've decided what you are storing, and what use you intend to make of the data, you are ready to start designing the database. Much of this can be done away from the computer.

What fields do you need?

You must break the data down into the smallest units (fields) that you will want to store, search or sort on.

If you are setting up *names*, you would probably break the name into three fields – *Title, First name* (or *Initials*) and *Surname*. This way you can sort the file into Surname order, or search for someone using the First name and Surname.

If you are storing *addresses*, you would probably want separate fields for *Town/city, Region* and/or *Country*. You can then sort your records into order on any of these fields, or locate records by specifying appropriate search criteria. For example, using *Town/ city* and *Country* fields, you could search for addresses in Washington (Town/city), USA (Country) rather than Washington (Town/city), UK (Country).

When planning your database, take a small sample of the data you wish to store and examine it carefully. This will help you confirm what fields will be required.

How big are the fields?

You must also decide how much space is required for each field. The space you allocate must be long enough to accommodate the longest item that might go there. How long is the longest surname you want to store? If in doubt, take a sample of some typical names (Anderson, Johnston, Mackenzie, Harvey-Jones?) and add a few more characters to the longest one to be sure. An error in field size isn't as serious as an error in record structure as field sizes can be expanded without existing data being affected.

ORGANISE!

This is very important! Take note! **Organise** your data before you start. Decide **what** you want to store, and **what** you want to do with it. Work out what **fields** are required (for sorting and searching).

You can edit the structure of your table if necessary – but hunting through existing data to update records is time consuming, so it's best to get it right to start with!

It is *very important* that you spend time organising and structuring your data *before* you start to computerise it – it'll save you a lot of time and frustration in the long run!

——— 1.9 Normalisation of data ———

As well as deciding what you need to store, you also want to minimise any data duplication as far as possible. For example, in the library scenario you may want to keep a record of the name, address and contact details of the publishing company for each book you hold. You could keep this information in the same table as the book detail as illustrated below.

Title	Author	Category	Library Code	Number held	Publisher	Publisher Address	Publisher Telephone Number

We have already touched upon the fact that this approach could present some basic problems, the most obvious ones being:

● *Effort to maintain your data* – keeping the data up to date could result in a lot of work as the same publisher fields are in many book records. A change in the telephone number of a publisher would result in many fields having to be updated.

● *Size* – your database would end up much larger than necessary because all of the publisher detail would be repeated many times.

● *Accuracy* – having to key the same detail in several times can easily lead to errors

The solution to this kind of problem is to use a process called *normalisation*. As a result of normalisation, you end up organising your data fields into a group of tables, which can easily be linked when and as required.

The simple solution to the problem highlighted above is to create two tables – one for the book detail, and one for the publisher detail. In each table you would need a Publisher ID (or Publisher Code) field, that would be used to identify each publisher uniquely. This field could then be used to link the tables when and as required.

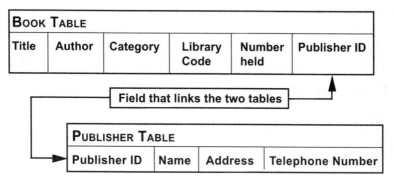

There are several benefits to this approach:

● Each set of publisher details is stored (and therefore keyed in) only once.

● The book table will be considerably smaller in size than it otherwise would have been.

● Should any of the publisher details change (phone number/address) you only have one record to update (in the Publisher table).

● If you wrongly identify a publisher in a record in the book table, you have only one field to correct, rather than all of the publisher's fields.

1.10 Chapter summary

In this chapter we have covered the following points:

● What a database is and what it might be used for (there are many other examples throughout the book).

● Database jargon that might be new to you, but that will become part of your language as you use databases.

● Access Objects – the basic components of an Access database.

● System requirements and installation procedures (if you are buying a new computer and Access software you could get the package pre-installed).

● The importance of planning and organising your data.

● The procedure known as normalisation.

2

IN, OUT and HELP

───── 2.1 Aims of this chapter ─────

This chapter will explain how to get Access 7 up and running. It will describe what you see on the Access screen and the menu structure used. The on-line help system will be introduced and some tips will be provided to help you locate the assistance you require as quickly as possible. Finally, the procedure for closing down Access 7 will be described. The examples in this book are based on running Access 7 under Windows 95.

───── 2.2 Getting into Access 7 ─────

Starting Access 7 is very similar to starting any other application. You really have two options available.

● The **Start** menu

● The **Microsoft Office Shortcut Bar**

When you start Access (using either method) you must decide whether you are going to create a new database, or are opening an existing one. In the instructions that follow, we are going to create a new database as we go into Access. This database will then be used throughout the book to explain many of the functions and features.

— 2.3 Starting from the Start menu —

1. Click the **Start** button on the Taskbar

2. Choose **Programs**

3. Click **Microsoft Access**

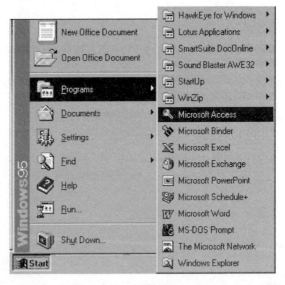

The Access 7 copyright screen will appear on your screen for a few seconds, followed by the **Microsoft Access** dialog box.

This dialog box gives you the option to create a new blank database, create a database using a Database Wizard (see Chapter 10 for details on Database Wizards), or open an existing database.

4. Choose **Blank Database** and click **OK**

5. You then arrive at the **File New Database** dialog box.

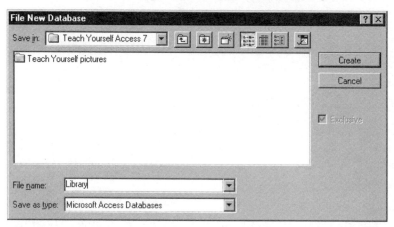

You must now decide where you want to store your database (*My Documents* is the default).

As with other Microsoft packages, a temporary filename is suggested for your database – in Access these follow the pattern db1, db2, db3 in each working session. You need to replace the temporary name with a name that means something to you, and reflects the contents of your database.

6. If you are working through the project in this book, I suggest you call it *Library* (as we are setting up a library database)

7. Once you have named your database click the **Create** button

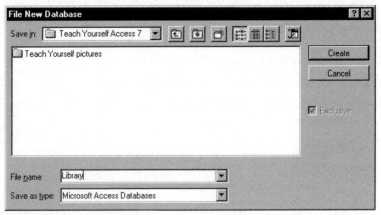

8. This takes you through into Access, with your *Library* database window displayed

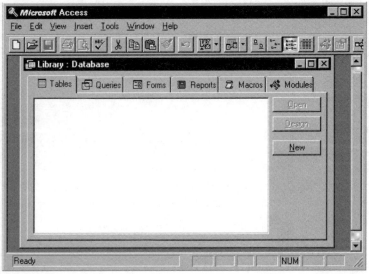

9. You have arrived safely in Access with your new database ready for you to work on

—— 2.4 Starting from the Shortcut Bar ——

As an alternative to using the **Start** menu on the Taskbar, you could use the **Microsoft Office Shortcut Bar** (if you've installed the office suite).

1. Click the **Start new document** tool 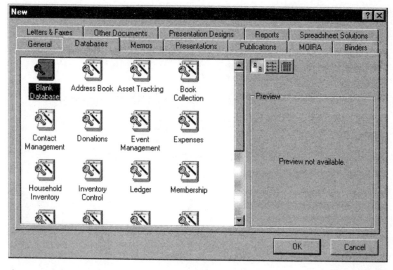 on the Shortcut Bar

2. At the **New** dialog box, choose the **Databases** tab

3. Select **Blank Database** (the other icons represent Wizards which are discussed in Chapter 10)

4. Click **OK**

Access is started, the copyright screen appears for a few seconds, and you arrive at the **File New Database** dialog box.

5. Specify where you want your database to be stored

6. Give your database a name, e.g. *Library* if you are working through the project in this book

7. Click the **Create** button

You will find out how to set up the Objects in your database later in this book (Chapters 4 through to 12). At this stage you should take a look at the Access screen, the menus and the on-line help and start to get used to the look and feel of the application.

2.5 The Access screen

If you are familiar with other Windows packages, many of the items on the Access screen will appear familiar to you. A brief overview of the main areas follow, so we all know what's what!

You should be able to identify the following areas within the **Access Application** window:

● Application Title Bar (where it says **Microsoft Access**)

● **Application Minimise, Maximise/Restore** and **Close** buttons (to the right of the Application Title Bar)

● Menu Bar (immediately under the Application Title Bar)

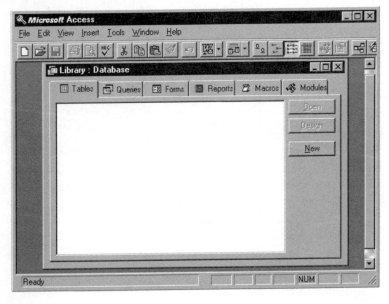

- Tool Bar (under the Menu Bar)
- Status Bar (at the bottom of the **Application** Window)
- **Database** window
- Database Title Bar
- **Database Minimise, Maximise/Restore** and **Close** buttons

These areas will be referred to often during the course of this book, and in any other publications you read.

2.6 The menus

There are seven menus in the **Access Application** window. You can use these to initiate any function or feature. Have a browse through the menus to get an idea of the features available in Access – some items may be familiar to you, some will be new.

As you work with different Access Objects, the menu bar will change and the options within each menu may vary.

The **File** menu, **View** menu and **Tools** menu are illustrated here:

You can display a menu list and select menu options using either the mouse or the keyboard.

Using the Mouse

Click on the menu name to display the list of options available in that menu, then click on the menu item you wish to use.

Using the Keyboard

You will notice that each menu name has an underlined character in it. You can open a menu by holding down the [Alt] key on your keyboard and pressing the appropriate letter, e.g. [Alt]–[F] will open the **File** menu, [Alt]–[I] will open the **Insert** menu.

Each item in a menu list also has a letter underlined in it. You can select an item from the menu list either by pressing the appropriate letter on your keyboard, or using the up and down arrow keys on your keyboard until the item you want is selected, and then pressing the [Enter] key.

Once a menu list is displayed, you can press the right or left arrow keys on your keyboard to move from one menu to another.

To close a menu without selecting an item from the list, either click the menu name again, click anywhere off the menu list or press the [Esc] key on your keyboard.

In addition to the menus, many of the commands can be initiated using the toolbars, keyboard shortcuts or shortcut menus. Each of these areas will be covered as you progress through the book.

———————— 2.7 I need Help!! ————————

Access is a big application, with lots of potential for most database designers and users. To complement this you will find a comprehensive on-line Help system. The on-line Help covers everything you are likely to need to know about Access in the near (and distant) future. Getting in and out of the Help system is easy – finding the answer that you are looking for gets quicker with practice.

You can get into the Help system in a number of ways but the easiest way into Help to begin with is either through the **Microsoft Access Help Topics** option in the **Help** menu, or by pressing the [F1] key on your keyboard.

When you are in the on-line Help system, read the instructions on each screen very carefully – they tell you exactly what to do.

There are four starting points to choose from:

● **Contents** tab

● **Index** tab

● **Find** tab

● **Answer Wizard** tab

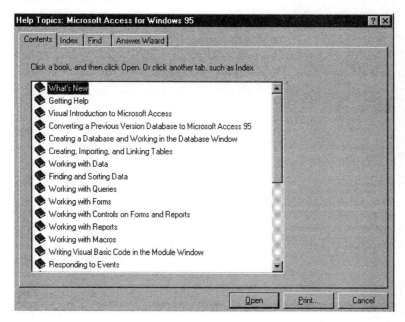

The starting point you choose is very much a case of personal preference.

Contents tab

From the **Contents** tab you can browse through the Help system, following any topic that appeals to you. This is a good starting place when you're new to Access, as you can explore and get a feel for what is available.

Just follow the prompts on the screen:

1. Select a **Book**, and click **Open**

2. Select a **Topic** and click **Display** or **Print**

Index tab

The **Index** tab gives an alphabetical listing of all the topics that are indexed within the Help system – this list is pretty long, and will, at least in the early stages of using Access, contain a lot of things that are unfamiliar to you. You can search for specific categories of information from the Index tab. The Index is particularly useful if you know the name of the topic that you are looking for, and want to get directly to the appropriate Help pages, without meandering through other pages.

Find tab

The **Find** tab allows you to search for words and phrases held within the Help system rather than look for a particular topic or category of information. This option provides a *very* long list of words you can search for. The first time you use the Find tab the **Find Setup Wizard** runs to set up your word list – I suggest you stick to the recommended options and follow the prompts on the screen to set up your list.

Answer Wizard tab

The **Answer Wizard** will probably be one of your main ways into Help once you've started to get used to the terminology. The trick with this one is to be able to phrase your question in such a way that the system is able to provide a selection of appropriate answers.

Questions like 'How do I print a table' or 'How do I save a record' provide a relevant list of topics to choose from. If a question doesn't come up with what you are looking for, reword the question and try again.

This one can be a bit hit and miss to begin with, but becomes more useful as you get used to things.

You can access the Answer Wizard directly by choosing **Answer Wizard** from the **Help** menu, or by pressing the [F1] key on your keyboard.

Tooltips

You will also find Help available on screen as you are using Access. Point to any tool on a toolbar, and pause.

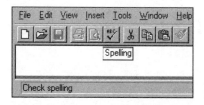

A Tooltip will appear to explain the function of the tool you are pointing to. In addition, a brief explanation of the tool's purpose will also appear on the Status Bar.

Help tool

At the end of most toolbars, you will find a Help tool ▣. You can use this tool to find out about areas of your screen, toolbars, menu items and so on.

To get help using the Help tool, click it, then do one of the following:

● Open a menu and select an item

● Click on another tool

● Click on another screen area, e.g. a **Database Object** tab in the **Database** window

A small panel will appear giving a brief description of the function of the item you select or click.

To cancel the Help tool without clicking on a menu, tool or screen area:

● Press the [Esc] key on your keyboard

   or

● Click the Help tool again

—— 2.8 Closing your database ——

When working within Access you can close your database without closing the application itself.

To close the database:

● Click the **Close** button ▣ on the **Database** window Title Bar

—————— 2.9 Leaving Access ——————

When you have finished using Access you must exit the package properly – **do not** just switch off your computer!!

● Choose **Exit** from the **File** menu

or

● Click the **Close** button 🗵 on the **Application** Title Bar

—————— 2.10 Chapter summary ——————

In this chapter we have concentrated on the following areas:

● Getting into Access using the Task Bar and the Microsoft Office Shortcut Bar.

● The Access Application window and the identification of the various areas therein.

● Utilising the menu structure using the mouse and the keyboard.

● The on-line Help system and the various options available to help you to find the assistance you need.

● How to close Access down successfully when you've finished working with it.

3

DATABASE DESIGN

3.1 Aims of this chapter

This is where the real work begins! In this chapter you will learn
how to design a database. We will discuss drawing up a task list
and working out what fields we need, identify field types and
discuss field properties. We will then consider how to minimise
the duplication of data and discuss how the tables relate to each
other within the database. Finally we will discuss how to create
new and open existing database files.

3.2 The project

The main project in this book is the setting up of a Library
database. The database will contain details of the books we have
on our shelves, the authors, the publishers, and so on. We will
limit the scope of the project to handling books, publishers and
authors – library members' details and details of books borrowed
will not be included at this stage.

Before you start working on the computer, there are three things you should do:

● Draw up a list of what is required from your database. Work out what you want to be able to do with your database. What tasks do you want to perform with it?

● Identify the fields required. Analyse the tasks and identify the data items (fields) you need to set up.

● Normalise your data to minimise redundant data – data that is duplicated unnecessarily. Duplication in a database results in three main problems:

◆ Changes require lots of effort

◆ The database ends up a lot bigger than it needs to be, wasting disk space

◆ More errors! If you key the same data in many times it is very easy to make mistakes.

— 3.3 Draw up a list of requirements —

The first thing you must do is sit down and think! Before you start to do anything on the computer, work out what it is that you intend to do with your database. Make a list of all the things you want your database to be able to provide for you. What information do you want to record? What kind of questions will you want the system to provide answers to? What reports do you want to generate?

Using our Library database example, we might come up with the following list of things we'd like to be able to do:

● Record, update and edit details of all books held in the library – title, author, publisher, etc.

● Keep details of the different categories of book held, e.g. science, travel, cooking

● Hold publisher details – name, address, telephone number, etc.

● Give the physical location of the book in the library – row, shelf number, etc.

● Provide details about the author of the book

● Extract different sets of data, e.g.:
  ◆ a list of all travel books from a specific publisher
  ◆ a list of science and astronomy books by a given author

● Prepare and print reports on various things:
  ◆ details of books in specific categories
  ◆ lists of books from a given publisher
  ◆ lists of books by a particular author

● Ease of use – not too difficult for staff to use

Once you've established what you want to be able to do with your database, you can start to plan how it might best be set up.

There are several things to consider here. In our example we want to record details of the books, publishers and authors of the books in our library. We want to be able to work with the data easily, without all the staff needing to become computer "whizz kids" and we want to be able to extract selective details from our database and print out attractive reports! Sounds good!

──3.4 Identify the detail required──

You must now work out what detail you will need to store to enable your Access database to fulfil the requirements you have identified for it.

The best way to do this is to consider each task individually, and write down what data items you think you will need for that task. A data item is simply a single piece of information about the thing you are working with – the book, author or publisher in our case. Include any notes that may be useful as you are working on your design. It's usually easy to think of the first few things you need, then it becomes harder as the list gets longer.

Write down the data items you come up with, and edit the list as you go through the process.

The use of a simple form can be handy here. Below are suggestions of what might be required for the eight tasks we have identified for the Library database.

Task 1: Record, update and edit details of all books held in the library – title, author, publisher, etc.

Detail	Description	Notes
ISBN	Unique reference	Primary Key
Title	Book title	
Author	Personal details	Name, date of birth, date of death, nationality, specialist area, any other information The information would be best held in a separate table, linked to the book table through the AuthorID. This approach would reduce unnecessary duplication of detail (which should mean a smaller database, with fewer errors).
Publisher	Contact details	Name, address, phone number, fax number, e-mail address The information would be best held in a separate table, linked to the book table through the PublisherID. This approach would reduce unnecessary duplication of detail and help promote accuracy.
Category	e.g. Science, History, Music, Cookery	The categories could be held in a separate Categories table and detail would be 'looked up' from the book table
Location	Row and shelf number	
Copies	Number held	
Pub. Year		
Price		
Reference or Lending	Identifies reference or lending book	

Task 2: Keep details of the different categories of book we hold, e.g. science, travel, cooking

Detail	Description	Notes
CategoryID	Unique identifier	Primary Key
Category Name	Description of category	eg Science, History, Travel

Task 3: Hold publisher details – name, address, telephone number, etc.

Detail	Description	Notes
PublisherID	Unique identifier for each	Primary Key
Publisher Name		
Publisher Address		
Publisher Phone Number		
Publisher Fax		
Publisher e-mail address		

Task 4: Give the physical location of the book in the library – row, shelf number, etc.

Detail	Description	Notes
Row Number ID		
Shelf ID		

Task 5: Provide details about the author of the book

Detail	Description	Notes
AuthorID	Unique identifier for each	Primary Key
Surname		
Firstname		
Date of Birth		
Date of Death		
Nationality		
Speciality		
Notes		

Task 6: Extract different sets of data from your database

● Ensure that table structure is broken down into the fields you want to sort and select on.

● Try to think of all the questions you might want to ask of your data, and set up the fields required when you specify the table structures. For example, if you want to be able to query your data to find out the titles of all the books you hold by a particular author, together with the publisher name and the year of publication, you will need to have a *Book Title* field, an *Author Name* field, a *Publisher* field and *Year Published* field somewhere in your database.

● Relational database structures are easy to edit, so it is possible to add, delete or edit fields that you make an error in at the set up stage. However, a bit of forward thinking at this stage can minimise the number of amendments that you will need to make in the future.

Task 7: Prepare and print reports on various things

● Ensure that table structure includes the fields required for the reports.

● Areas to consider here are as per the notes in the previous task.

● If you want to be able to produce a report grouping the books you hold under the heading *Publisher*, perhaps with an author grouping within the publisher grouping, the book titles sorted in ascending alphabetical order, and the total number of books held from each publisher displayed, you must have the fields required set up in the structure of your tables.

Task 8: Ease of use – not too difficult for staff to use

● Include validation checks on data to help reduce errors.

● Design a user friendly interface for staff.

Once you have completed this stage of the planning process, you can work out what fields will be required, how best to group the fields into tables and how the tables will be related to each other.

—————— 3.5 Normalisation ——————

When deciding on the tables required, you should consider how best to group the fields to minimise the duplication of data throughout the database – this is what is meant by the process of *normalisation*.

Table structure

Using the information contained in the lists above, we might decide to record all the Book details in one table, but use a separate table for the Publisher detail and a separate table for the Author detail. We could also have a fourth table that contains a list of the different categories of book. You must decide which fields should be in each table.

You must also decide what kind of data will be held in each field – will it be text, numbers, date, currency and so on.

Primary Key

You must also decide which field (or combination of fields) would uniquely identify each record held within each table. This field (or group of fields) would be the *Primary Key* for the table. In our example a single field in each table would be sufficient for the Primary Key. In the *Book* table the *ISBN* would be different for each book, so this would make the ideal Primary Key for the *Book* table. Each Publisher would have their own ID, so this would be the field to choose for the Primary Key, and each Author would have their own ID, so the *AuthorID* would be the field to choose for the Primary Key in the *Author* table.

By breaking the detail down into four tables in this way, the details on each publisher would only need to be recorded once, in the *Publisher* table. The details on each author would also only need to be recorded once, in the *Author* table. The *Category* names would only need to be entered once. Within the *Book* table, you would simply need to enter the publisher, author and category codes in the appropriate fields and these would facilitate the link through to the other tables when required.

Details of the book's location within the library could be held in the main book table – there is no real benefit to be derived from placing this in a separate table.

Book table

The field list for the *Book* table (together with possible data types) would therefore be:

BOOK TABLE		
Field Name	**Data Type**	**Notes**
ISBN	Text	Primary Key
Title	Text	
AuthorID	Number	
PublisherID	Number	
CategoryID	Number	Look up Category Name field
Row Number	Number	
Shelf Number	Number	
Number Held	Number	
Publication Year	Number	Year only held
Price	Currency	
Reference or Lending	Text	

Publisher table

The field list for the *Publisher* table (with data types) would be:

PUBLISHER TABLE		
Field Name	**Data Type**	**Notes**
PublisherID	AutoNumber	Primary Key
Publisher Name	Text	
Publisher Address	Text	
Publisher Phone Number	Text	
Publisher Fax	Text	
Publisher e-mail address	Text	

Author table

The field list for the *Author* table (with data types) would be:

AUTHOR TABLE		
Field Name	**Data Type**	**Notes**
AuthorID	AutoNumber	Primary Key
Surname	Text	
Firstname	Text	
Date of Birth	Date	
Date of Death	Date	
Nationality	Text	
Speciality	Text	
Notes	Text	

Category table

We can use another table to identify the category of book. By doing this, the full name of the book category would only need to be keyed in once, but it could be 'looked up' from the *Book* table at any time using a 'Look Up' option through the *CategoryID*.

CATEGORY TABLE		
Field Name	**Data Type**	**Notes**
CategoryID	AutoNumber	Primary Key
Category name	Text	

So, by using some forward planning, we have reached the stage where we have decided that a database consisting of four tables is just what we need for this situation.

3.6 Relationships

The *Book* table in our database is related to each of the other tables within the database as indicated below.

Table	Related to	Joining Fields	Type of Relationship
Publisher	Book	PublisherID	One-to-many
Author	Book	AuthorID	One-to-many
Category	Book	CategoryID	One-to-many

The type of relationship in each case is one-to-many (this is the most common type of relationship between tables). One record in the *Publisher* table may be related to many records in the *Book* table – our library contains lots of books from each publisher. One record in the *Author* table may be related to many records in the *Book* table – many authors have written more than one book. One record in the *Category* table may be related to many records in the *Book* table – there are many books in each of our book categories.

The tables are related to each other as shown in this diagram.

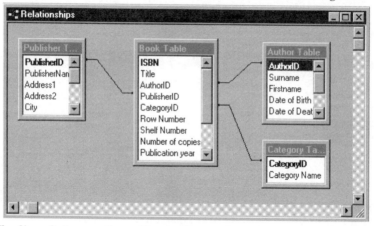

The lines between the tables indicate which fields are related to each other – these are called *join lines* in Access.

The Primary Key in each table is displayed in bold – the relationships we need are between the Primary Key of the *Author*, *Publisher* and *Category* tables and the appropriate *foreign key* (the *Primary Key* viewed from another table) in the *Book* table.

You will learn how to define the table structures and set the relationships in Chapter 4.

——3.7 Creating a new database——

We are now ready to define the structures for our tables. If you have not created your library database file and do not have Access currently up and running, go into Access as described in Chapter 2 and create a database file called *Library*.

Create a new database from within Access

If you are already in Access, but have not yet created the *Library* database file:

1. Click the **New Database** tool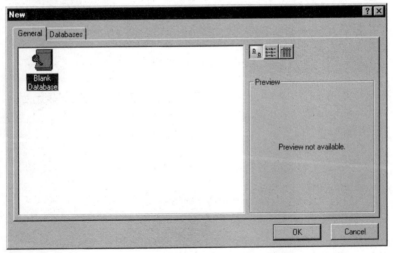
2. At the **New** dialog box, choose the **Blank Database** from the **General** tab
3. Click **OK**

4. Specify the folder you wish to save your database into
5. Give the database a name
6. Click **Create**

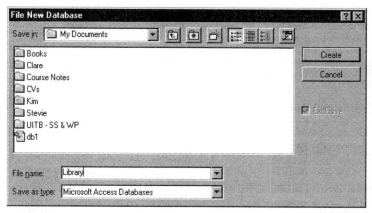

If you have set up your *Library* database, but have closed it or exited Access, you must open the database again to work on it.

—3.8 Opening an existing database—

If Access is not already up and running, start Access as described in Chapter 2. At the **Microsoft Access** dialog box, select the *Library* database from the list of existing databases. Click **OK**.

Your *Library* database will appear on your screen.

Open an existing Database from within Access

If Access is already running:

1. Click the **Open** tool 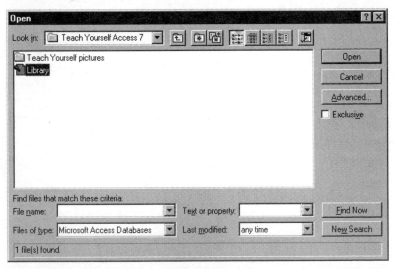 to display the **Open** dialog box.

2. Locate the folder that contains your database (probably *My Documents,* but you may have saved it somewhere else) and select the *Library* database from the file list displayed.

3. Click **Open** to open the database.

OPENING FROM THE FILE MENU

If the database you wish to open has been used recently, you may find it listed at the end of the **File** menu. To open a file from the recently used file list, open the menu, then click on the file name you require. The four most recently used files are listed at the end of the **File** menu.

Whether you have created a new database, or opened an existing one, the *Library Database* window should now be displayed on your screen.

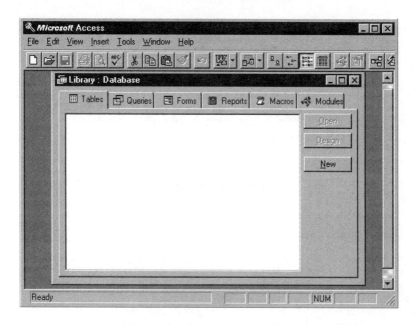

———— 3.9 Chapter summary ————

In this chapter we have tried to introduce you to the ground work required before you start to set up the tables in your Access database. We have discussed:

● Drawing up a list of requirements.

● Requirements analysis and field identification.

● Normalisation of data.

● Relationships between tables.

● Creating a new database file.

● Opening an existing database file.

4

TABLE DEFINITION

4.1 Aims of this chapter

Once you have worked out the database design it is time to start
setting up the table structures within your database. In this chapter we will look at the options available when defining the table
structure – whether you do it manually, or using a Wizard. We
will then set up the relationships between the tables we define.

4.2 Creating the table structure

1. Select the **Tables** tab within your **Database** window and click
   the **New** button.

2. At the **New Table** dialog box, select **Design View** and click
   OK.

Design view

Your new table is displayed in Design view on your screen. In Design view you can specify the field names, data types and any other properties you think would be useful.

The Design view window has two panes – an upper one where you specify the field name, data type and description, and a lower one where you specify the field properties. You can move from one pane to the other by pressing the [F6] key on your keyboard.

● To move from column to column in the upper pane, press the [Tab] key on your keyboard. You can also point and click with your mouse to move around the window.

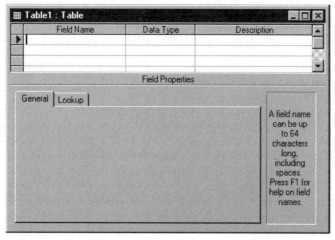

—— 4.3 Data types and properties ——

Data types

There are nine different data types to choose from when setting up your table structures. Brief notes on each type are given in the table below for your information. Most of your fields will probably be **Text**, with a few of the others used in each table depending on the type of data you wish to store.

Data Type	Usage	Size	Notes
Text	Alphanumeric data	up to 255 bytes	Default data type
Memo	Alphanumeric data	up to 64 Kbytes	Cannot be indexed
Number	Numeric data	1,2,4 or 8 bytes	
Date/Time	Dates and times	8 bytes	Values for the years 100 through to 9999
Currency	Monetary data	8 bytes	Accurate to 4 decimal places and 15 digits to the left of the decimal separator
AutoNumber	Unique long integer created by Access for each new record	4 bytes	Cannot be updated Useful for primary key fields
Yes/No	Boolean data	1 bit	Yes and No values, and fields that contain one of 2 values – On/Off, True/False
OLE Object	Pictures, graphs or	Up to 1 gigabyte OLE objects from other Windows applications	Cannot be indexed
Lookup	Lets you look up values in another table or from a combo box	The same as the Primary Key used to perform the look up	Choosing this option starts the Lookup Wizard to define the data type

Properties

You can customise each field by specifying different properties. These vary depending on the data type. The properties you will encounter are listed below:

Property	Data Type	Notes
Field Size	Text and Number	Text from 1 – 255 characters
	Number field sizes are: ♦ Byte (single byte) ♦ Integer (2-byte) ♦ Long Integer (4-byte) ♦ Single (4-byte) ♦ Double (8-byte)	Values: ♦ 0 – 255 ♦ -32,768 to +32,767 ♦ -2,147,483,648 to 2,147,483,648 ♦ -3.4 x 10^{38} to 3.4 x 10^{38} ♦ -1.797 x 10^{308} to +1.797 x 10^{308}
Format		Options depend on the data type
Decimal places	Number and Currency	Auto (displays 2 d.p. for most formats except General Number, where decimal places depend on the precision of the number) or Fixed – 0 to 15 d.p.
Input Mask	Text, Number, Currency and Date/Time	Uses special characters to show the type of input allowed, and whether or not input is required See notes on input masks below
Caption		For display on forms and reports
Default Value	All data types except Memo, OLE Object and AutoNumber	
Validation Rule		You can supply an expression that must be true when you enter or edit data in this field
Validation Text		You can specify the message to appear on the screen when a validation rule is not met
Required		Set to Yes if data must be entered
Allow zero length	Text and Memo fields	
Indexed	Text, Number, Currency, Date/Time and AutoNumber types	Indexing speeds up access to its data – fields that will be sorted or queried on should be indexed

Input Mask character descriptions

0	Digit (0-9), entry required. Plus (+) and Minus (-) signs not allowed
9	Digit or space. Plus (+) and Minus (-) signs not allowed
#	Digit or space, Plus (+) and Minus (-) signs allowed
L	Letter (A-Z), entry required
?	Letter (A-Z)
A	Letter or digit, entry required
a	Letter or digit
&	Any character or space, entry required
C	Any character or space
<	Convert following characters to lower case
>	Convert following characters to upper case
!	Causes input mask to fill from right to left when characters on the left side of the input mask are optional
\	Causes the following character to be displayed as a literal character, i.e. \L is displayed as L. Entry required.

Additional notes

● An input mask can contain up to three sections, separated by a semi-colon, i.e.

99/99/00;0;_

● The first part specifies the pattern for the mask itself.

● The second part specifies whether or not any literal display characters are stored with the data. The default value is 0 meaning that they are; 1 means that only the data is stored.

● The final part sets the character used to display spaces in the input mask at data entry. The default is the underline character. If you want to use a space, enclose it in quotes, i.e.

99/99/00;0;" "

—— 4.4 Defining the Category table ——

Using the field list tables we drew up earlier, we can set up the structure of our tables in Access. We will set up the *Category* table first. This table *must* be set up before the *Book* table as the Book table will look up data from this table.

The records in the *Category* table are very small – only two fields – one containing the *CategoryID* and one containing the *Category name*.

CategoryID

1. In the **Field Name** column, key in the field name:

   CategoryID

2. Press the [Tab] key to move along to the **Data Type** column and set this to **AutoNumber** (click the **drop down arrow** to display the list of options and select **AutoNumber**)

3. Press [Tab] to move along to the **Description** column and enter a field description if you wish

The description is optional – complete it if you think it might be useful. You can key in a description for any field you want to clarify the purpose of. Anything you key in the description column will appear on the status bar during data entry to that field.

Category name

Enter the category name details in the second row of the upper pane.

1. In the **Field Name** column, key in the field name:

   CategoryName

2. Press the [Tab] key to move along to the **Data Type** column and set this to **Text**.

   The default field size for a Text data type is 50 characters. This is more than is required for a category name, so this property could be reduced – 25 would be big enough.

3. Press [F6] to move to the lower pane (or click with the mouse) and change the field size from 50 to 25

CATEGORY TABLE			
Field Name	**Data Type**	**Properties**	**Notes**
CategoryID	AutoNumber	Primary Key	
CategoryName	Text	Field Size = 25	

Establishing Primary Key status

The *CategoryID* field is the primary key for this table – i.e. its unique identifier.

● To establish Primary Key status, click the **Primary Key** tool
  🔑 when the insertion point is anywhere in the *CategoryID* field row in the upper pane.

Note that the **Index** property is automatically set to **YES (No Duplicates)** when a field is given Primary Key status.

Save and close the table design

1. Click the **Save** tool 🖫 on the Design toolbar. If this is the first time you've saved the table the **Save As** dialog box will appear.

2. Give your table a suitable name

3. Click **OK**

4. Click ❌ to close the **Table Design** window

Your new table will be listed on the **Tables** tab in the **Database** window.

———4.5 Defining the Book Table———

Once the *Category* table has been set up we can set up the *Book* table. Data types and the Properties for each field have been suggested.

1. Select the **Tables** tab within your **Database** window and click the **New** button

2. At the **New Table** dialog box, select **Design View** and click **OK**

Setting up the ISBN field

1. In the **Field Name** column, key in the field name – *ISBN* in our case

2. Press the [Tab] key to move along to the **Data Type** column and set this to **Text**

3. Press [Tab] to move along to the **Description** column and enter a field description if you wish

Field properties

1. Press [F6] to move to the lower pane (or click with the mouse) and change the field size from 50 to 20

2. Set the **Required** property option to **YES** – each book must have an ISBN

3. Press [F6] to return to the upper pane

Establishing the Primary Key status

The *ISBN* field is the primary key for this table.

● To establish Primary Key status, click the **Primary Key** tool when the insertion point is anywhere in the *ISBN* field row in the upper pane

Complete the structure for the rest of the book table following the guidelines in the table below. See notes below regarding the CategoryID field specification.

BOOK TABLE			
Field Name	**Data Type**	**Properties**	**Notes**
ISBN	Text	Field Size = 20 Required = Yes	Primary Key
Title	Text	Field Size = 50	
AuthorID	Number	Long Integer	
PublisherID	Number	Long Integer	
CategoryID	Number	Long Integer	Value will be 'looked up' in the category table
Row Number	Number	Integer Validation Rule >=1 and <=40 Validation Text *"Enter a number between 1 and 40"*	Rows numbered 1 - 40, if an incorrect entry is made, display the validation text message
Shelf Number	Number	Integer Validation Rule >=1 and <=6 Validation Text *"Enter a number between 1 and 6"*	Shelves numbered 1 - 6, if an incorrect entry is made, display the validation text message
Number Held	Number	Integer	
Publication Year	Number	Integer	As we are entering only the year of publication, use Number data type
Price	Currency		
Reference	Yes/No		
Lending	Yes/No	Default value = Yes	
Picture	OLE Object		Illustration for book

● Press [Tab] or use the mouse to move from column to column.

● Press [F6] or use the mouse to move between the upper and lower panes.

Any field that you think you will want to sort on or query should be indexed. Indexing a field enables Access to sort or select on that field faster than it would be able to do on a non-indexed field.

CategoryID Field

1. Select **Lookup Wizard...** from the **Data Type** list. This invokes the Lookup Wizard to walk you through the set up process

2. At the first dialog box, choose '**I want the lookup column to look up the values in another table or query**' and click **Next** (you want to look up the values in the Category table)

3. Select the *Category* table from the list and click **Next**

4. Move the *CategoryName* field from the **Available Fields:** list to the **Selected Fields:** list (select the *CategoryName* field in the **Available Fields:** list and click the top button between the two lists to move it over) and click **Next**

In our *Book* table, we want to display the *CategoryName* **not** the *CategoryID* that links the two tables.

5. Adjust the width of the column if necessary (instructions are on the screen) and click **Next**

6. Leave the **Hide key column** checkbox selected. Access will use the *CategoryID* field to link the two tables, but won't display the code on the datasheet or form. It will display the category as Science, Cooking, Travel, etc. instead. It is often easier to work in this way, rather than have ID numbers displayed

7. Check the suggested column label, and change it if you wish – I suggest you change it to *Category*, as that is the data that will be displayed in the column. The column label will appear in the **Caption** property row for the *CategoryID* field in the **Table Design** window

8. Click **Finish**

9. You will be prompted to save the table on completion of the

Wizard. I suggest that you choose '*Yes*' (even if you have not set up the whole table structure yet) and name it *Book table*

The completed structure should be similar to the illustration below.

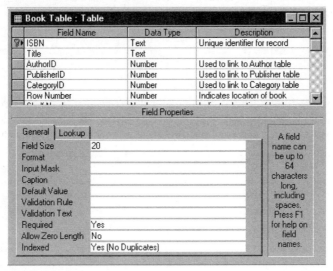

Save the table design

● When you have finished setting up the whole table remember to **Save** 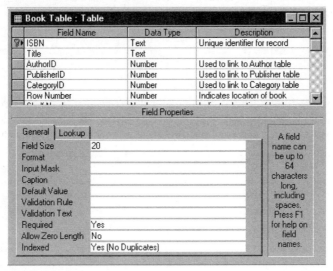 the *Book* table and close the **Table Design** window.

If you have already saved an earlier version of the table, clicking the *Save* tool will replace the old version of the table on your disk with the new one.

—— 4.6 Defining the Author table ——

The Author table is set up in a similar way. Set up the design for the Author table following the guidelines below.

AUTHOR TABLE			
Field Name	**Data Type**	**Properties**	**Notes**
AuthorID	AutoNumber	Long Integer	Primary Key
Surname	Text	Size = 20 Indexed = Yes Duplicates OK	
Firstname	Text	Size = 20 Indexed = Yes Duplicates OK	
Date of Birth	Date/Time	Pick a Format Input mask = 99/99/00	Type in the code, or click the Build button beside the Input Mask field and work through the Wizard
Date of Death	Date/Time	Pick a Format Input mask = 99/99/00	Type in the code, or click the Build button beside the Input Mask field and work through the Wizard
Nationality	Text	Size = 25 Indexed = Yes Duplicates OK	
Speciality	Text	Size = 20 Indexed = Yes Duplicates OK	Enter description: "Main area of author's work"
Notes	Memo		

● **Save** 🖫 the *Author* table and close ✕ the **Table Design** window.

——————— 4.7 Table Wizard ———————

The last table structure to be set up is the *Publisher* table. This is essentially just a name and address table which could be set up manually, just as we have set up the other three tables. We could also consider using a Wizard to help automate the setting up of this table. Wizards can save you time when it comes to setting up a table structure – there are several provided with often-used structures for different situations, including name and address structures.

1. On the **Tables** tab of the **Database** window click **New**

2. At the **New Table** dialog box, choose **Table Wizard**

3. Click **OK**

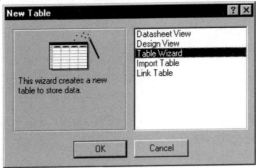

At the **Table Wizard** dialog box:

4. Select the **Business table** classification

5. Choose **Suppliers** from the list of **Sample tables:** (the publishers are the suppliers for our library)

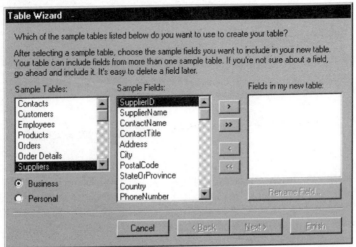

SEE WHAT THE WIZARD OFFERS

At some stage, have a browse through the tables listed in both the Business and Personal classifications. You can save yourself a lot of time setting up a basic table structure by using a Wizard.

---

6. Select the fields required (one field at a time) from the **Sample Fields:** list and add them to the **Fields in my new table:** list (click the top button between the two lists)

7. To add all the fields from the **Sample Fields:** list to the **Fields in my new table:** list, click the second button

8. To remove a field from the **Fields in my new table:** list, select it and click the third button , or click the last to remove all the fields from the **Fields in my new table:** list

Your list should be similar to the one shown below:

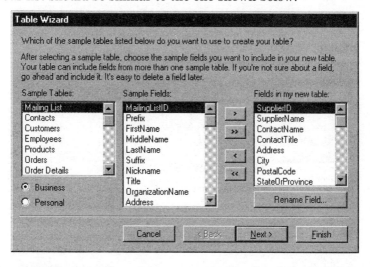

As our table is really going to contain details of the Publishers we use, we could change some of the field names to reflect this.

Renaming a field

To rename a field, e.g. *SupplierID* to *PublisherID*:

1. Select *SupplierID* in the **Fields in my new table:** list
2. Click the **Rename Field** button

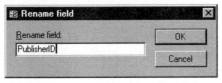

3. Enter a new name in the **Rename field** dialog box
4. Click **OK**

Do this for any other fields you wish to rename – *SupplierName* could become *PublisherName*, *StateOrProvince* could become *County*.

5. When you are satisfied with the field names, click the **Next** button to move on to the next step in the Wizard
6. The Wizard automatically suggests a name for your table – edit the table name if necessary – *Publisher* table would perhaps be a more suitable name than *Suppliers* in this case

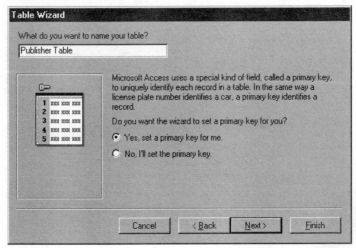

7. At the **Primary Key** options, let Access set the Primary Key for you – the *PublisherID* field will be made the Primary Key

8. Click **Next** to move on to the next step

Checking relationships

The dialog box displays the relationships between your new table and any tables you have already set up in your database. Sometimes Access relates the tables automatically using the field names and properties, other times it fails to make a relationship and you must tell it what relationships exist.

The *Publisher* table should be related to the *Book* table in a one-to-many relationship – one record in the *Publisher* table may have many related records in the *Book* table as we may have several books from the same publisher.

If Access has not made the relationship, or if you wish to check that Access has made the correct relationship between your tables:

1. Select the row that specifies the relationship status to the *Book* table

2. Click the **Relationships...** button

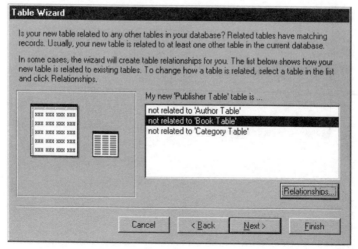

3. At the **Relationships** dialog box, check the relationship status. The second one should be selected – one record in the *Publisher* table may be related to many in the *Book* table

4. Select this option if necessary

5. Click **OK**

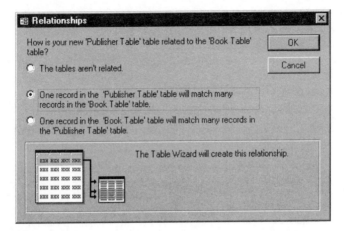

6. Click **Next** to move on to the final step in the Wizard

When you reach the checkered flag, you know you have reached the final step in your Wizard.

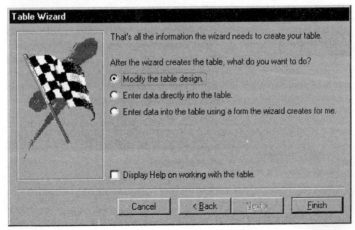

7. Select **Modify the Table Design** (this will allow us to check that the field properties are set up the way we want them)

8. Click **Finish**

You will be taken through to the **Design** window for the *Publisher* table you have just set up.

● Move through the fields, checking the properties in the lower pane as you go.

THE MASKED DANGER!

Beware of any Input Masks set up for the postcode, phone and fax numbers. These will follow American conventions and will cause problems when we try data entry using British (or European) layout.

Deleting Input Masks

Delete any input masks from the lower pane for these fields.

1. Click anywhere in the appropriate field row in the upper pane

2. Move to the lower pane (press [F6])

3. Select the **input mask** detail (click and drag over it)

4. Press the [Delete] key on your keyboard

You may also notice detail in the **Caption** field property for some fields – the phone, fax and e-mail fields for example. Anything keyed into the Caption property will appear as a label on any Form using that field – see Chapter 7 on Forms Design.

5. **Save** ▣ the changes you have made to the design of the *Publisher* table and **Close** ☒ the table

You will be returned to your **Database** window, where all four tables are listed on the **Tables** tab (illustrated overleaf).

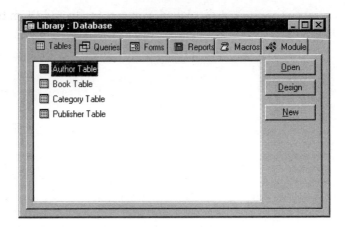

4.8 Relationships

Before moving on you should check the relationships between the tables in your database, and modify any that are not correct.

● To check the relationships between your tables, click the **Relationships** tool.

The **Relationships** window opens, displaying the tables in your database and any relationships that are already established.

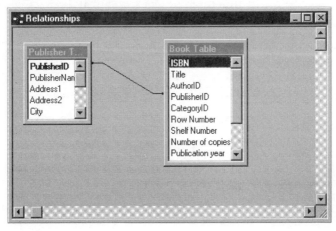

If all the tables are not displayed, you can easily add them to the **Relationships** window.

1. Click the **Show Table** 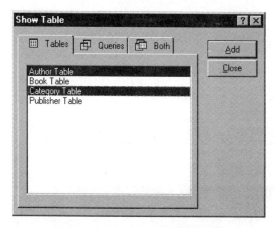 tool to display a list of the tables in your database

2. Select the table (or tables) you wish to add to the **Relationships** window and click the **Add** button

You can add several tables to the **Relationships** window at the same time if you wish.

If the tables are listed next to each other in the **Show Table** dialog box, select the first table you wish to add, then point to the last table you wish to add, hold the [Shift] key down and click – all the tables within the range will be selected.

If the tables you wish to select are not next to each other, click on the first one you want to select, then hold the [Ctrl] key down while you click on each of the other tables required.

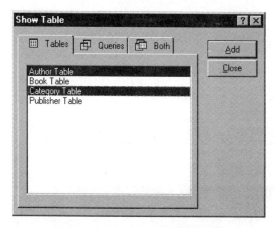

3. Click the **Close** button once you have added your tables

Your **Relationships** window will contain all the tables required and any relationships will be displayed.

The lines running between the tables are called *join lines*. The join lines run between the fields linking the tables. Access will often create the link between tables automatically – especially if

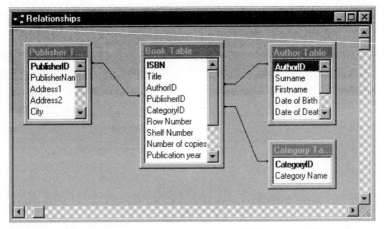

there are fields with the same name in different tables. Access will assume that where two tables have the same field name in them, these fields are the ones that link the tables.

Deleting and creating join lines

You can delete join lines and create other join lines as required.

To delete an existing relationship:

1. Click on the join line you wish to remove to select it

2. Press the [Delete] key on your keyboard

3. Respond to the prompt as required

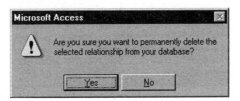

To create a relationship:

4. Click on the field you wish to relate to another table to select it

5. Drag the selected field and drop it onto the field you wish to link it to in the other table

6. At the **Relationships** dialog box, click **Create** to establish the relationship

7. If you want to check the type of relationship that will be created, click **Join Type...** to view the options in the **Join Properties** dialog box

8. Change the type if necessary

9. Click **OK**

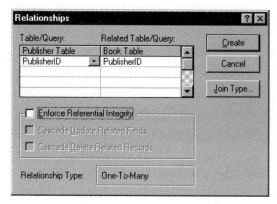

——— **4.9 Chapter summary** ———

In this chapter we have discussed the alternative ways of defining the tables within your database. We have discussed:

● Defining a table in Design view.

● Data types available.

● Data properties.

● Defining a table using a Table Wizard.

● Checking, creating and deleting relationships between tables.

5

DATA ENTRY and EDIT

5.1 Aims of this chapter

In this chapter we will start to enter data into our tables. Working
in Datasheet view, we will look at the various options for data
entry and edit together with display options for the datasheet.
As an alternative to Datasheet view, we will use a simple form
for data entry and edit.

PROJECT DATA

If you are working through the library project in this book,
key in the data suggested for all four tables. You will find
suggested data for each of the tables in Appendix 1.

—— 5.2 Data entry in Datasheet view ——

If you are working through the project in this book, you should be in Access with your *Library* database open. The four tables that we defined in the previous chapter will be listed on the **Tables** tab of the **Database** window.

I suggest you do the *Publisher, Author* and *Category* tables before the *Book* table – this way you'll have the necessary codes for the *PublisherID, AuthorID* and *Category* fields in the *Book* table. Data entry is very easy for the most part. You simply open the table and key in the data – using the [Tab] key or the mouse to move from field to field. As you are keying in the data, look out for the features mentioned below.

● To open a table in **Datasheet** view, double click on the name, or select the table required on the **Tables** tab and click **Open**.

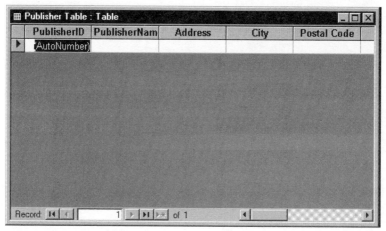

In Datasheet view, your table looks similar to a spreadsheet layout – each record is presented in a row and each field is in a column.

● To move forward through the fields press the [Tab] key.

● To move backwards through the fields press [Shift]–[Tab].

● Or click in the field you want to move to using the mouse.

Publisher table

AutoNumber

The *PublisherID* field has the AutoNumber data type – this field will be completed automatically by Access; you cannot enter any data into it.

● Press the [Tab] key to move from column to column, entering your publisher data.

When you complete one record (when you reach the last column):

● Press [Tab] to move on to the first column of the next record.

PublisherID	PublisherName	Address1	A
1	Hodder & Stoughton Ltd	338 Euston Road	
2	Borthwick-Henderson	Applewood House	Apple\
3	Westward Lock Ltd	18 Clifftop Street	
4	Softcell Press	One Softcell Rise	
5	Christy Corporation	20 E 103rd Street	
6	Arrows Publications	Randall House	10 Ca`
7	Harry Cousin Ltd	10-23 Frosty Road	South
8	Beaver Books Ltd	7 Squirrel Lane	
9	Darling Kinghorn Ltd	2 Herbert Street	
10	City Publishing Company Ltd	7 Queen Street	
11	Scrambler Publications Ltd	6-9 Prince Street	
12	BPU Publications	Europa House	Queer
13	Outreach College Press	Wilson Way West	

Publisher Table : Table

Record: 13 of 15

You may notice, as you key in your data, that the record you are currently writing to has a pencil icon in the row selector area to the left of the record.

Author table

Input mask

When entering data to the *Author* table, note the effect of the input mask on the *Date of Birth* and *Date of Death* fields. When you enter data into these fields, the pattern set for the data appears and you just key in the figures.

Access also carries out its own validation tests on data that you key into a date field. If you try entering a date like 30/02/60 you will get an error message to indicate the date is not recognised.

AuthorID	Surname	Firstname	Date of Birth	Date of Death	Natio
1	Peterson	Brian			Englis
2	McDonald	Alastair	12/01/36		Scotti
3	Jackson	Marion	24/06/55		Englis
4	Adamson	Pauline			Austra
5	Duncan	Wilma	04/07/38		Ameri
6	Ferguson	John	03/04/03	05/10/88	Irish
7	Jackson	Allan	10/12/40	02/ /	
(AutoNumber)					

Record: 7 of 7

Description

If you look at the status bar when entering data into a field for which you keyed in a description during table definition, you will notice that the description text appears in the status bar when you are in that field, e.g. the *Speciality* field for the *Author* table.

Firstname	Date of Birth	Date of Death	Nationality	Speciality	N
Brian			English	Romantic Fiction	
Alastair	12/01/36		Scottish	Poetry	
Marion	24/06/55		English	Travel	
Pauline			Australian	Children's Fiction	
Wilma	04/07/38		American	Travel	
John	03/04/03	05/10/88	Irish	Gardening	
Allan	10/12/40	02/10/93	Scottish	Travel	

Record: 7 of 7

Main area of author's work   NUM

Book table

Category field

When the insertion point is in the *Category* field:

1. Click the **drop down arrow**
2. Select the name required from the list (the entries in the list have been looked up in the *Category* table)

	Title	AuthorID	PublisherID	Category	Row Num
	In & Out Stories	8	11	Children's Fiction	
	Castaways	8	6	Children's Fiction	
	The 2nd World War	3	14	History	
	Teach Yourself Access 7	13	1	Computing	
	Campfire Cooking	20	8	Cooking	
	Garden Shrubs	6	8	Cooking	
	African Drums	14	1	Craft	
	Bits & Bytes	13	2	Education	
	West Highland Way	7	1	Family	
	Hamsters at Home	8	6	Foreign	
	Giant World Atlas	20	13	Gardening	
	Easy Internet	17	2	Geography	
	The Night Sky	2	13	Health	
▶	Bread and Biscuits	11	7	Cooking	

Record: |◄| ◄| 14 |►| ►I| ►*| of 20

Validation rules and validation text

Check out your validation codes in the *Row Number* and *Shelf Number* fields by entering a shelf number over 40 and a row number over 6.

Yes/No fields

In the book table we defined the **Yes/No** data type for the *Reference* and *Lending* fields. On entering data in Datasheet view notice that they are displayed as checkboxes.

● To register a 'Yes' there must be a tick in the box.

● To register a '**No**' leave the box empty.

You can toggle the status of this field by clicking on the checkbox.

Default Value

Notice that the *Lending* field has been selected automatically for each record. This is because we set the Default Value to **Yes** when we defined the table.

OLE Object

In the *Book* table we defined an OLE Object data type for the *Picture* field to allow us to insert a picture that reflected the style, mood or subject of the book.

To insert an object into an OLE Object field in Datasheet view:

1. Choose **Object...** from the **Insert** menu

2. At the **Insert Object** dialog box select the object type required – in this example **Microsoft ClipArt Gallery**

3. Click **OK**

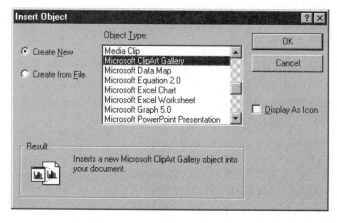

4. Select the picture you wish to use in your OLE field and click **Insert**

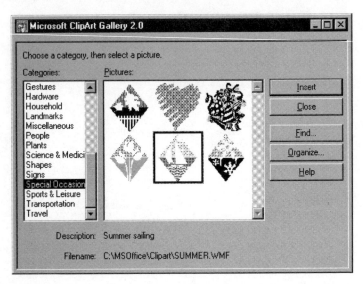

In Datasheet view the picture is not displayed, but the name of the application from which the Object came – Microsoft ClipArt Gallery – is.

—— 5.3 Datasheet and Design view ——

If you discover a problem with your table design, you can move from Datasheet view to Design view to fix it.

● To move from Datasheet view to Design view, click the **Table view** tool ![icon] on the toolbar.

If you make any changes to the design of your table, you must remember to save them. Be careful not to make any design changes that will result in your losing data that you need, e.g. reducing the size of a field too much.

● To move back into Datasheet view, click the **Table view** tool ![icon] on the toolbar.

——— 5.4 Editing in Datasheet view ———

Moving through your table

We have already discussed the fact that you can move within and between records using the [Tab], [Shift]–[Tab] keyboard techniques, or by pointing and clicking in the desired field using the mouse.

At the bottom left of the table window, you will find a set of tools designed to help you move through your table in Datasheet view.

● The record number field tells you which record the insertion point is currently in, and to the right of this you will find the total number of records in your table.

● The arrows to the right ▶ and left ◀ of the current record number allow you to move forwards and backwards through your records, one at a time.

  The current field remains constant as you move up or down through your records – although you are moving from one record to another, the same field in each record is selected.

● The arrows further to the right ▶▌ and left ▐◀, move you through to the last record in your table, or back to the first record in your table.

● To go to a specific record number, select the record number in the record number field, enter the record number you wish to go to and press [Enter].

Editing the field contents

If you spot an error in Datasheet view, you must position the insertion point within the field you wish to edit, and make whatever changes are required.

You can use the scroll bars (horizontal and vertical), or the record selector buttons to locate the record you need to update. Once the record has been located, the simplest technique is to click within the field that needs to be changed and insert or delete data as necessary.

If you use the [Tab] or [Shift]–[Tab] keyboard techniques to move through fields that contain data, the contents of a field are selected when you move on to it.

● To replace the selected data within a field, simply key in the new text – whatever you key in will replace the original data.

● To delete the data in the field press the [Delete] key when the old data is still selected.

● To add or delete data *without* removing the current contents of the field, you must deselect the field contents before you edit.

To deselect the field contents, either click within the field using your mouse, or press the [F2] key on your keyboard. Once the data is deselected you can position the insertion point and insert or delete as required.

Adding new records

Regardless of which record your insertion point is currently in, the **New Record** button or tool takes you to the first empty row at the end of your table to allow you to add a new record.

—— 5.5 Formatting in Datasheet view ——

When working in Datasheet view, there are a number of formatting options you might like to experiment with.

Formatting the datasheet affects the whole table, not just the row or column the insertion point is in.

To change the font

1. Choose **Font...** from the **Format** menu
2. Complete the dialog box with details of the font style, size and attributes required
3. Click **OK**

To change the cell format

1. Choose **Cells...** from the **Format** menu
2. Specify which gridlines you wish to show, the gridline colour, the background colour and cell effect required
3. Click **OK**

To change row height

1. Choose **Row Height...** from the **Format** menu
2. Specify a row height, or select the **Standard Height** checkbox
3. Click **OK**

You can also use your mouse to change the row height.

1. Move the mouse pointer over the row selector area (the grey column to the left of the fields)
2. Position the mouse pointer over the dark line between two rows – you should get a black double-headed mouse pointer
3. Click and drag up or down until the required height is reached

To change column width

1. To change the column width of a particular column, place the insertion point anywhere within the column

2. Choose **Column Width...** from the **Format** menu

3. Specify the width required or select **Standard Width**

4. Click **OK**

Alternatively, you can let Access work out the best size for the column by choosing **Best Fit**.

You can also resize the column width using the mouse.

1. Position the mouse pointer over the dark line to the right of the field name of the column you wish to change the width of – you should get a black double-headed mouse pointer

2. Click and drag right or left to make the column to the left bigger or smaller

To get Access to do a **Best Fit** sizing, double click the dark line to the right of the field name in the column you wish to resize.

───── 5.6 Data entry in Form view ─────

As an alternative to entering data into a table in Datasheet view, you could use Form view.

In Datasheet view, each record is displayed in a row, each field in a column. As many fields and records are displayed in the table window as will fit.

In Form view, the fields are arranged attractively on the screen (you can design forms to resemble paper forms you actually use) and one record is displayed at a time. Form view is often considered more user friendly than Datasheet view.

AUTOFORM

Access has a useful tool that builds a simple form automatically – AutoForm. You do not need any form design skills to use AutoForm – we'll look at designing custom forms in Chapter 7.

AutoForm from the Database window

To create an AutoForm for a table:

1. Select the table you wish to use from the **Tables** tab in the **Database** window

2. On the Database toolbar, click the **drop down arrow** to the right of the **New Object** tool

3. Choose **AutoForm**

The table you selected is displayed using a simple form layout.

You can move around in Form view in the same way as you did in Datasheet view:

● Press [Tab] or [Shift]–[Tab] to move from field to field, or click in the field you want to input or edit.

● Use the record selector buttons to move from record to record, or to the first or last record in the table.

● To go to a specific record number, select the record number in the record number field, enter the record number you wish to go to and press [Enter].

● Click the **New record** button to get a blank form on which to enter new data.

● If necessary, use the scroll bars to display parts of the form that are not displayed in the window.

The data you enter or edit in your form in Form view will be stored in the table on which the form is based. Even if you opt not to save the form itself, the data will still be stored.

Any field types defined as an OLE Object (e.g. the *Picture* field in the *Book* table) will have the picture displayed in Form view, whereas in Datasheet view the name of the source application is displayed.

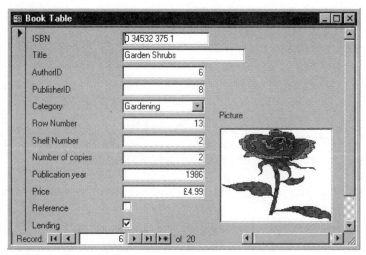

AutoForm from Datasheet view

If you have been working on your table in Datasheet view, you can easily change to Form view using the AutoForm tool.

In Datasheet view, there is also a **New Object** tool on the Table Datasheet toolbar. Choose **AutoForm** from the drop down list to display your datasheet in Form view.

Changing Views

When working with a form, you have three views of your table you can choose from – Design, Datasheet and Form. To change views:

1. Click the **drop down arrow** to the right of the **Table View** tool

2. Click on the view required

Saving your Form

If you want to save your form:

1. Click the **Save** tool on the Form view toolbar

2. At the **Save As** dialog box, either accept the default form name, or edit it as required

3. Click **OK**

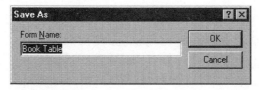

If you close your form without first saving it, Access will ask you if you want to save the form.

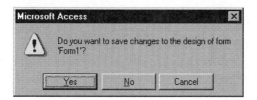

If you choose **Yes**, you will be taken to the **Save As** dialog box as described above. If you choose **No**, the form will close without being saved. If you click **Cancel**, you will be returned to Form view.

If you save your form, it will be listed on the **Forms** tab in the **Database** window. You can open the form again from this tab at any time – either double click on the form name or select the form name and click **Open**.

5.7 Chapter summary

In this chapter we have considered the main options for entering and editing data in your tables. In this chapter you have found out about:

● Opening your tables in Datasheet view.

● Entering and editing data in Datasheet view.

● Moving between records.

● Adding new records.

● Formatting the datasheet.

● Moving between the different table view options.

● Creating a simple form using AutoForm.

● Saving the Form.

6

TABLE MANIPULATION

——— 6.1 Aims of this chapter ———

In this chapter you will learn how to manipulate the structure of your table – add fields, delete fields, change field properties and move fields. You will also learn how to add and delete records in Datasheet view, hide and unhide columns, freeze and unfreeze columns and print from Datasheet view.

—— 6.2 Changing the table structure ——

To edit the table structure you must take your table into Design view. You can do this from the **Database** window if you select the table you need to edit on the **Tables** tab, and click **Design**.

Alternatively, if you are already in Datasheet view, you can go into Design view by clicking the **Table View** tool .

Adding a new field

● If the new field is to go at the end of the structure, scroll through the rows until you reach the empty row under the existing fields. Enter the field name, data type and properties as required.

To add a new field between two existing fields:

1. Place the insertion point in the upper pane anywhere within the field that will be below your new field

2. Click the **Insert Row** tool — a new empty row is inserted above the one the insertion point is in

3. Enter the field name, data type etc. as required

Deleting a field

1. Place the insertion point in the upper pane within the field to be deleted

2. Click the **Delete Row** tool

3. Respond to the prompt – choose **Yes** to delete the field, **No** if you've changed your mind

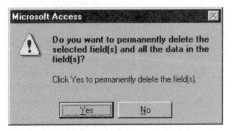

DELETE WITH CARE

Be careful when you delete fields – any data held within that field in your records will be lost.

Changing the field properties

1. Place the insertion point in the upper pane within the field whose properties you are going to edit

2. Press [F6] to move to the lower pane

3. Edit the properties as required

4. Press [F6] to return to the upper pane

When changing a field size, watch that you don't end up losing data. If you reduce the field size, any record that has data in that field in excess of the new field size will have the extra characters chopped off!

Primary Key

To change the field that has Primary Key status:

● In the upper pane, place the insertion point in the field that you want to take Primary Key status. Click the **Primary Key** tool.

To remove Primary Key status, and *not* give it to any other field:

● In the upper pane, place the insertion point in the field that has Primary Key status and click the **Primary Key** tool.

Renaming a field

You can rename a field in either Design or in Datasheet view.

To rename a field in Design view:

● Edit the name you wish to change in the first column in the upper pane.

To rename a field in Datasheet view:

1. Double click on the field name you want to change in the **Field Name** row

2. Edit the field name as required

3. Press [Enter] or click in the record detail area

――― 6.3 Rearranging the fields ―――

You can move the fields in either Design view or Datasheet view.

Design View

1. In the upper pane, click in the row selector bar to the left of the field you wish to move

2. With the mouse pointer over the selector bar area, drag and drop the field into its new position – you will notice a thick dark horizontal line that indicates the position that the field will move to

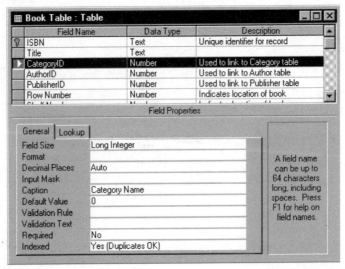

To keep the fields in their new position you must save the design before you close your table.

Datasheet view

1. Select the field by clicking in the **Field Name** row above the field you wish to move

2. With the mouse pointer in the **Field Name** row, drag and drop the field into its new position – you will notice a thick dark vertical line indicating the position that the field will move to

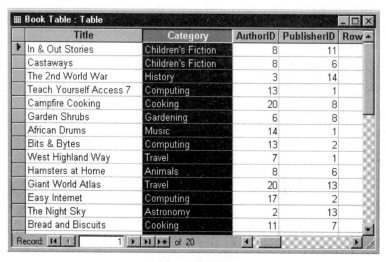

When you close your table, you will be asked if you wish to save the layout changes to your table.

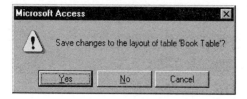

Choose **Yes** to save the changes, **No** to close the table without saving the changes, or **Cancel** to return to the table to do some more work.

6.4 Editing the datasheet

Adding new records

When adding new records you add them to the end of the list of existing records:

1. Click the **New Record** tool 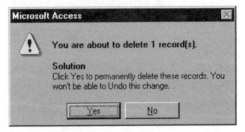 to move through to the first empty row under the existing records

2. Key in your data

Deleting records

1. Place the insertion point within the record you wish to delete

2. Click the **Delete Record** tool

3. Respond to the delete prompt as required – choose **Yes** to confirm the deletion; choose **No** if you've changed your mind

Microsoft Access

> You are about to delete 1 record(s).
>
> **Solution**
> Click Yes to permanently delete these records. You won't be able to Undo this change.
>
> Yes   No

6.5 Hiding columns

When working in Datasheet view, the number of fields displayed and the horizontal scroll required to move from the first field to the last field in a record can make it difficult to view the data you require. You may find yourself scrolling back and forward checking and double checking field contents.

If you aren't interested in the contents of some fields for the time being, you can hide the fields you don't need.

HIDDEN NOT DELETED

When you hide columns, they aren't deleted but simply hidden from view.

To hide a field (or fields) you must first select the field (or fields) you want to hide.

To select a single field

1. Move the mouse pointer to the top of the field you wish to hide – into the **Field Name** row

2. The mouse pointer should become a solid black arrow pointing downwards

3. Click to select the column

To select adjacent columns

There are two methods to choose from when selecting several adjacent columns:

● Click and drag in the **Field Name** row (when the mouse pointer is a solid black arrow) across the columns to be selected

or

1. Select the first field by clicking in the **Field Name** row above the required column

2. Scroll through the columns until you can see the last column in the group you require

3. Hold the [Shift] key down and click in the **Field Name** row at the top of the last column to be selected

All the fields between the first and last column identified will be selected.

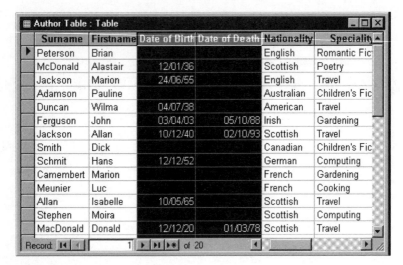

4. To hide the selected columns open the **Format** menu and choose **Hide Columns**

To display hidden columns

When you want to display the columns again

1. Choose **Unhide Columns...** from the **Format** menu

2. Select the fields you want to display and click **Close**

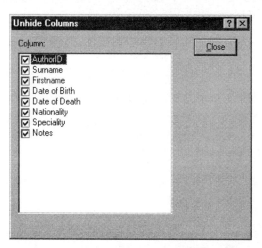

6.6 Freeze columns

When you freeze a column or columns, they become the leftmost columns in your table. Columns that are frozen do not scroll off the screen – they remain static while the other columns in your table scroll in and out of view.

To freeze a column or columns

1. Select the column(s)

2. Open the **Format** menu

3. Choose **Freeze**

If the column(s) you choose are not at the left side of the table, they will be moved there.

If you need to freeze columns that are not adjacent to each other, select and freeze them one by one until you have built up the arrangement of frozen columns required. Once the columns are frozen you can scroll the other columns in and out of view as required – the frozen ones will remain at the left. On your screen, you will notice a dark vertical line between the frozen columns and unfrozen columns.

To unfreeze a column or columns

● Choose **Unfreeze All Columns** from the **Format** menu

The columns that are unfrozen remain to the left of the table – you have effectively moved the fields and placed the fields that were frozen at the beginning of the table.

Closing the table

When you close your table, you will be asked if you want to save the changes to the layout of your table.

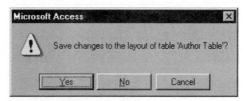

If you choose **Yes**, the new field order will be saved, if you choose **No** the fields will remain in the order they were before you froze them.

—— 6.7 Printing from Datasheet view ——

Using the formatting options discussed in Chapter 5 (changing font and cell attributes), and those discussed in this chapter (hiding columns, moving columns and freezing columns) you can format your datasheet ready for printing.

Print preview

Before printing your table from Datasheet view, it is recommended that you do a Print Preview to check that it will look okay on the page.

● Click the **Print Preview** tool

A preview of your datasheet will be displayed. In Print Preview the Print Preview toolbar is displayed. You can use this to work with your table.

● To send your table to the printer from **Print Preview**, click the first tool on the toolbar.

● To zoom in on your datasheet, click the second tool on your toolbar – you click the same tool to zoom out again (you can also zoom in and out if you place the mouse pointer over the preview page and click).

● The third and fourth tools give you the option of viewing one or two pages at a time while in Print Preview.

● The **Zoom Control** field lets you select the magnification of the zoom in percentages (the default options toggle the zoom between **100%** and **Fit** – where you see the whole page at a time).

● The **Close** tool returns you to Datasheet view. If you use the close button at the top right of the preview window, your table will be closed and you will return to the **Database** window.

You can preview a table from the **Database** window, as well as from Datasheet view.

● To preview a table from the **Database** window, select the table on the **Tables** tab and click the **Print Preview** tool. When you close your preview window you will be returned to the **Database** window.

Margins and orientation

If you need to change the margins or the orientation of your table before you print it, you must go into the **Page Setup** options. To view the **Page Setup** options:

1. Open your table in **Datasheet** view

2. Select **Page Setup...** from the **File** menu

On the **Margins** tab of the dialog box, you can change the top, bottom, left or right margins. You can also specify whether or not you want to print the field name (column headings) at the top of each field.

On the **Page** tab, you can change the **Orientation** (portrait or landscape), the **Paper Size** and **Source** details, and the **Printer** details.

Print

You can print your datasheet from Print Preview or from the datasheet itself. To send one copy of the table to the printer:

● Click the **Print** tool 🖫 on either the table datasheet toolbar or the print preview toolbar.

To select a group of records for printing:

● Click and drag down the row selector column (the grey column to the left of the records) in Datasheet view until you've highlighted the records required.

If you need to print more than one copy of your datasheet, or specific pages, or a group of records you have selected:

1. Choose **Print...** from the **File** menu

2. Specify the options you require in the **Print** dialog box.

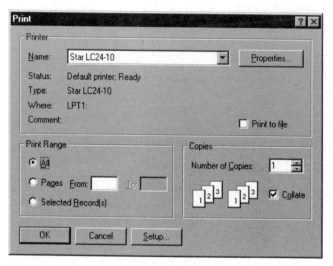

You can also print a table directly from the Database window:

1. Select the table you want to print on the **Tables** tab of the **Database** window

2. Click the **Print** tool

6.8 Chapter summary

In this chapter you have concentrated on a number of techniques that are useful when working with datasheets.

You have learnt how to:

- Add and delete fields in an existing table.
- Change the field properties of existing fields.
- Rearrange the fields within your tables.
- Rename fields.
- Add new records to a table.
- Delete records from a table.
- Hide and unhide columns.
- Freeze and unfreeze columns.
- Preview your table prior to printing.
- Print your table.

7

FORMS DESIGN

7.1 Aims of this chapter

In this chapter we will look at Forms design. Forms are not essential for data entry and edit, but they offer a much more user friendly view of the data held in your tables than Datasheet view does. You can design your forms to look like the paper forms you use, or you can design them with a view to making your data entry and edit tasks easier.

AutoForm, the manual design of forms and Form Wizard will all be addressed in this chapter.

7.2 AutoForm

AutoForm was introduced in Chapter 5, where we discussed data entry and edit techniques.

You can generate a simple form based on any table or query in your database using AutoForm – see **section 5.6 Data entry in Form View** to recap on how you create an AutoForm.

Your AutoForm form has a simple columnar display with the field names used as labels to describe the contents of each field. If you entered a **Caption** in the **Field Properties** pane for any field when defining the table structure, the caption appears as the label describing the field contents, rather than the field name.

The design of your AutoForm can be edited using any forms design techniques discussed in this chapter – you can move the fields, resize them, change the labels, delete fields, and so on.

To edit the layout of your form you must take it into Design view by selecting *Design View* from the **Table view** options available.

When you leave a form which was created using AutoForm, you are given the option to save the form. If you save the form it will be listed on the **Forms** tab in the **Database** window. Even if you do not save your form, any records you added or edited will be stored in the table on which the form was based.

Experiment with AutoForm using the tables in your database.

7.3 Form Design

You can design your own form layout, selecting the fields you want to display and arranging them attractively on your screen.

We will design a simple form to display our Publisher details.

Starting the Form design process

1. Select the **Forms** tab in the **Database** window and click **New**

2. At the **New Form** dialog box, select **Design View**

3. Choose the *Publisher* table as the table or query from which the object's data comes

4. Click **OK**

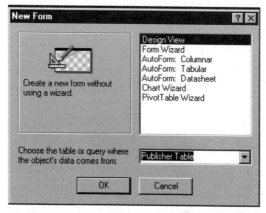

The **Form design** window will appear on your screen. In addition to the grid on which you design your form, there should also be a **Field List** displaying the field names from the table on which you are building the form, and a **Toolbox** that is used to help you design the form.

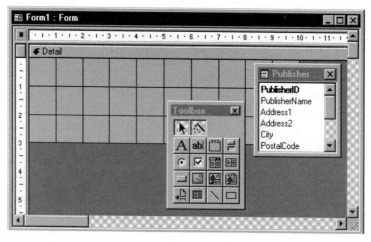

● If there is no Field List, click the **Field List** tool ▣ to display it – this tool toggles the display of the Field List.

● If there is no Toolbox, click the **Toolbox** tool ⚒ to display it – this tool toggles the display of the Toolbox.

The Toolbox is actually a toolbar that can be moved around the screen like any other toolbar. If it is not docked and is obscuring your work, click and drag its title bar to move it to a new position, or drag the toolbar to a 'dock' at the top or the bottom of the screen (if you dock it right or left, not all the tools are visible).

Form areas

The main areas in a form are the:

● **Detail** area

● **Form Header and Footer** area

● **Page Header and Footer** area

The Detail area is the part of your form in which most of the detail from your table or query will be displayed.

The Form Header and Footer areas appear above and below the detail area for each record when you take your form back into Form view.

Form Headers and Footers are used for titles or instructions you wish to appear above and below each form.

● Open the **View** menu and choose **Form Header/Footer** to toggle the display of this area on and off.

The Page Headers and Footers appear at the top and bottom of each page, should you opt to print your form out. Page Headers would be used for main headings and column headings that you want to appear at the top of each printed page. The Page Footer is often used for page numbers, dates, or any other information you want to display at the foot of each page.

● Open the **View** menu and choose **Page Header/Footer** to toggle the display of this area on and off.

> ## WARNING!
>
> If you enter any data into the Form or Page Header or Footer areas, and then opt not to display the area, the data you entered will be lost.

In the form we are about to design, we need a Form Header/Footer area:

● Open the **View** menu and choose **Form Header/Footer** to display the area.

———————— 7.4 Labels ————————

If you have instructions or headings to key into your form, you use the Label tool. We need a heading in our Form Header area – 'Book Publishers'.

1. Click the **Label** tool A
2. Move the mouse pointer into the form header area (notice the mouse pointer shape ⁺**A**)
3. Click and drag in the **Form Header** area to draw a rectangle where you want your heading to go
4. Let go the mouse – the insertion point is inside the label field
5. Key in your heading
6. Click anywhere outside the label field

Create another label underneath the one you have just made. This one should contain the text:

Publisher name and address details

If you think the Form Header area is not deep enough for this label, you can resize it by clicking and dragging the bottom edge of the header area (the mouse pointer will change to a black double headed arrow when you are in the correct place). The header area will also deepen automatically if you enter a label field too deep for its current size.

Your design should be similar to the one below.

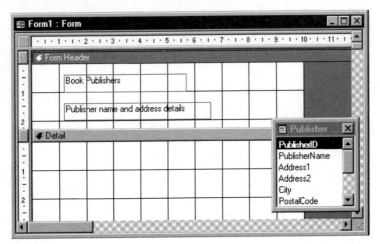

────── 7.5 Formatting fields ──────

The fields you have added can be moved, resized, formatted or deleted – so it's not critical that you get everything right first time.

To change the field attributes, you must select the field you want to work on.

● Click on the *Book Publishers* title to select it.

You will notice that a selected field has 'handles' around it – one in each corner and one half way along each side.

● To resize a field, click and drag a handle in the direction you wish the field to resize to.

- To move a field, position the mouse pointer over the edge of the field (not over a handle) and click and drag – the mouse pointer looks like a hand when you are in the correct place.

- To delete a field, select it, then press the [Delete] key on your keyboard.

Try making the Book Publishers heading font style Arial, font size 20, bold and text colour red! Now make the Publisher name and address details bold, italic and font size 12.

- To change the font size, colour, toggle bold, italics, underline, etc. experiment with the options on the **Formatting** toolbar when the field is selected.

If the data is too large for the field, resize the field as necessary. Your design should look something like the example below.

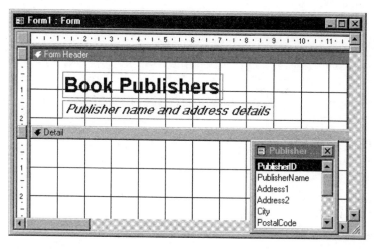

In the detail area of our form, we want to display the data held in the Publishers table – name, phone number, address, and so on.

- Deepen the Detail area ready for the fields you are about to insert into it. You can click and drag the bottom edge of the detail section to resize it.

If you want your form to be wider, you can click and drag the rightmost edge of it to resize it.

7.6 Text Boxes

To set up the design for the detail area we have to click and drag the fields required from the Field List onto the Detail area of our form. Once the fields are in the Detail area, we can position them, resize and format them as necessary. The fields we drag from the field list to the form are displayed as *text boxes.*

● Click and drag the *Publisher Name* field from the **Field List** and drop it on the detail area of your form.

You will notice that fields from the Field List consist of two parts – the leftmost part is the field label (either the field name or the caption if you entered one in the field properties), the rightmost part will display the actual data held in the field when you return to Form view.

Both components of the field are selected – if you move or delete the field the whole thing will be affected.

● Place the *PublisherID* field next to the *PublisherName* one. Your form should now look similar to the one below.

● Format the label of each field (the left part) to be font size 10 and bold – click on the leftmost part to select it, then use the Formatting toolbar to apply the formats required.

We are now ready to arrange the address details. This time, we want only one heading *Address* for all the individual address fields we will insert.

● Use the **Label** tool [A] and enter a label that says **Address** below the *PublisherName* field.

Arranged under this, we want the *Address1*, *Address2*, *City*, *County*, *Postalcode* and *Country* fields. However, as we already have an *Address* label, we do not require the individual field labels – so we can delete them.

1. Click and drag your first field over – probably *Address1*. To delete the label component, select the leftmost part of the field (click on it) and press the [Delete] key on your keyboard. The label should disappear but the rightmost part should remain

2. Do the same with the other address fields, and arrange them attractively on your form

3. Insert the *Phone*, *Fax* and *E-mail* fields to the right of the address detail

4. We don't need the Form Footer area on this form – click and drag its bottom edge up until it disappears

Your form should be similar to the one below.

5. Click the **Save** tool on the toolbar to save your form. At the **Save As** dialog box, give your form a suitable name and click **OK**

6. Take your form through into Form view to see how it looks. It should be similar to the one below

When you close your form, you will find its name listed on the Forms tab in the Database window.

7.7 Form Wizard

In addition to the manual design of forms, you could try out the Form Wizard when you need to design a form. The wizard takes you through the forms design process step by step, asking you questions on the way.

We are going to design a form displaying the *ISBN*, *Title* and *Category* fields from the *Book* table, the *AuthorName* details from the Author table, and the *PublisherName* from the *Publisher* table.

To start creating your form using Form Wizard:

1. Select the **Forms** tab in the **Database** window

2. Click **New**

3. At the **New Form** dialog box, choose **Form Wizard**

4. Click **OK**

At the first Form Wizard dialog box, select a table or query from which you want to include fields (you can include fields from more than one table or query on your form).

5. Choose the *Book* table and move the *ISBN*, *Title* and *CategoryID* fields from the **Available fields list:** over into the **Selected fields:** list

6. Select the *Author* table from the **Tables/Queries** list and add the *Firstname* and *Surname* fields

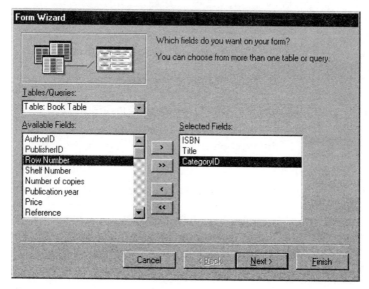

7. Finally, select the *Publisher* table from the **Tables/Queries** list and add the *PublisherName* field

The completed dialog box should look like this:

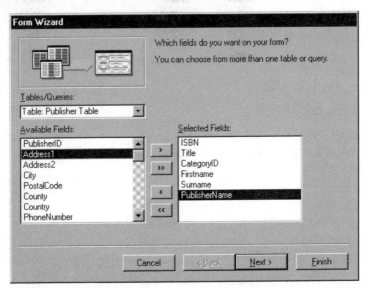

Now move on to the next step.

WORKING IN A WIZARD	
To move on to the next step	Click Next
To go back a step	Click Back
To exit the wizard without creating a form	Click Cancel
To create a form using the default options	Click Finish

8. Select the option you want to use when viewing your data. In this example, choose **By Book Table**, and **Single Form**

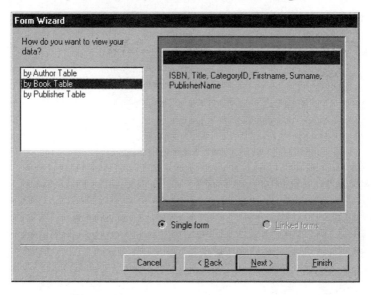

Move on to the next step.

9. Choose the layout you want to use for your form – **Columnar** in this example – and click **Next**

At the next step you can choose the style of your forms. The style determines the colours and design layout.

10. Pick one and move on to the next step

When you reach the checkered flag you are at the last step in the wizard.

11. Give your form a name (either accept the one suggested or key in your own – this name will appear on the **Forms** tab in the **Database** window)

12. Select **Open the form to view or enter information** and click **Finish**

Your form should look something like this:

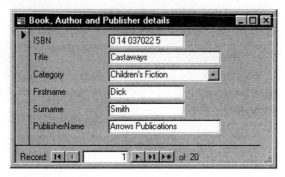

You can tab through the fields in your record using the [Tab] key on your keyboard, and move between records using the arrows at the bottom of the form.

When you close your form, you will find it listed on the **Forms** tab in the **Database** window.

If you would like your data displayed in a summary form, e.g. a list of books by author, or a list of all the books you have from each publisher, the Form Wizard can easily help you design the form required for this.

Further work with a Wizard

Work through the Form Wizard again selecting the following fields for your form. (You can include the *PublisherID* and/or *AuthorID* if you want to.)

Publisher table:	*PublisherName*
Book table:	*ISBN*, *Title* and *CategoryID*
Author table:	*Firstname* and *Surname*

1. When you get to the step where you are asked to select the option you want to use when viewing your data – choose **By Author** or **By Publisher**, whichever you wish

2. Select the **Form with subform** option – the *Publisher* or *Author* form will have a subform within it listing the book details

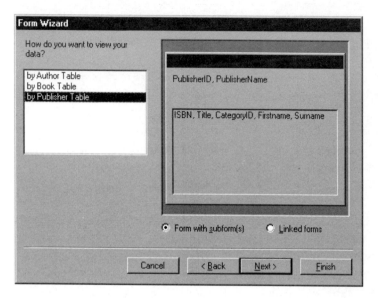

3. At the next step choose the tabular layout for your form

4. Continue working through the Wizard, specifying the style and names you want to use for your forms (either accept the default ones, or amend them to your liking). These form names will be listed on the **Forms** tab in the **Database** window

5. At the checkered flag, choose **Open the form to view or enter information** and click **Finish**

Two forms will be generated – your main form, either the publisher or author one, and the book subform.

Looking at your form you can use the lower set of record arrow buttons to move from one publisher record to another (or one author record to another).

If you have a long list of books you can use the upper set of record arrow buttons to move through the books in the list.

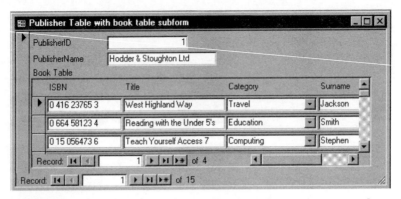

If you take the form through into Design view, you can see how this was set up.

The *PublisherID* (if included) and *PublisherName* fields, or *AuthorID* (if included) and *AuthorName,* are text boxes.

The lower section is a subform/subreport field. You can only create subform fields if the subform already exists – if you wanted to generate a subform field in a form manually, you would have to design the subform first.

The subform must be identified as the source of the data that will be displayed in that area of your main form. This is set up in the property options for that field.

● To view the property options, select the subform field and click the **Properties** tool 📑 on the **Form Design** toolbar.

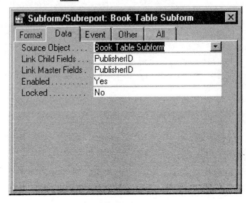

The subform/subreport property options are displayed in a dialog box. On the **Data** tab the source of the data and the linking fields are identified.

● Close the dialog box when you have finished looking at the properties.

7.8 Printing forms

Forms are usually used for data entry and edit on your computer. There may be times when you want to print your forms out – you could perhaps print out an empty form to send to someone for manual completion.

If you want to print out a form, you can do so using similar techniques to those used when printing out a datasheet.

1. Select the form you want to print on the **Forms** tab in the **Database** window

2. Click the **Print Preview** tool ▣ to preview the form, or click the **Print** tool ▣ to print out a copy

Or

● Open the form in Form view, and preview and print from there.

Access will fit as many forms as possible on the page size you have selected, so depending on the size of your form, you may have one or several forms printed out on the same sheet.

7.9 Chapter summary

In this chapter we have looked at different ways of designing your own forms. You have learnt how to:

● Create an AutoForm.

● Set up a simple form manually.

● Switch headers and footers on and off.

● Set up labels and text boxes.

● Use Form Wizard to generate forms for you.

● Print your forms.

8

SORT, FILTER and QUERY

8.1 Aims of this chapter

In this chapter, you will learn how to sort the records in your tables into the required order, find records within your table and filter the records to display those that meet specific criteria.

You will also learn how to create expressions to extract records that meet specific criteria from your table.

The techniques discussed in this chapter can be used on your tables in Datasheet view or in Form view.

8.2 Simple sort

It is very easy to sort the records in your table on a single field.

1. Open the table you are going to sort

2. Place the insertion point anywhere within the field you want to sort the records on

3. Click the **Sort Ascending** ![Sort Ascending icon] or **Sort Descending** ![Sort Descending icon] tool

● To sort the records in the *Book* table in ascending order on the *Title* field, open the *Book* table, place the insertion point anywhere within the *Title* field, and click the **Sort Ascending** tool.

The *Book* table, with the records sorted into ascending order on the *Title* field, is displayed below.

ISBN	Title	Category	AuthorID	Pu
▶ 0 412 32132 2	African Drums	Music	14	
0 412 46512 1	Bits & Bytes	Computing	13	
0 563 49124 5	Bread and Biscuits	Cooking	11	
0 345 12342 3	Campfire Cooking	Cooking	20	
0 14 037022 5	Castaways	Children's Fiction	8	
0 587 39561 0	Changing Skys	Astronomy	16	
0 576 26111 2	Crazy Comets	Astronomy	15	
0 482 31456 1	Easy Internet	Computing	17	
0 34532 375 1	Garden Shrubs	Gardening	6	
0 465 77654 3	Giant World Atlas	Travel	20	
0 45 469861 2	Hamsters at Home	Animals	8	
0 14 032382 3	In & Out Stories	Children's Fiction	8	
0 85234 432 6	Outdoor Adventures	Travel	12	
0 758 34512 1	Perfect Pizzas	Cooking	11	

Record: |◄| ◄ | 1 | ► | ►| | ►* | of 20

Saving changes

When you close a table that you have sorted, you will be asked if you want to save the changes.

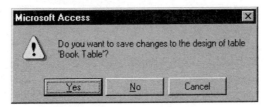

To save the records in the new, sorted order, choose **Yes**; if you don't want to save the changes, choose **No**.

8.3 Multi-level sort

If you want to sort your table on several fields, you must set up your sort requirements in the **Filter** dialog box.

You might want to sort your *Book* table into ascending order on *CategoryName*, and within each category you might want the books sorted into ascending order on *Title*. If necessary, open your *Book* table to try this out.

1. Open the **Records** menu and select **Filter, Advanced Filter/ Sort...**

2. In the upper half of the **Filter** dialog box the field list of the current table is displayed. Scroll through the list until you see your main sort field – in our case *CategoryID*

3. Double click on the field name – the field name will appear in the first column of the field row in the lower pane

4. Place the insertion point in the **Sort** row below the field name (you can move from pane to pane by pressing the [F6] key on your keyboard, or use your mouse). Either type the letter **a** to select **Ascending** order, or display the options available (click the **drop down arrow**) and choose **Ascending**

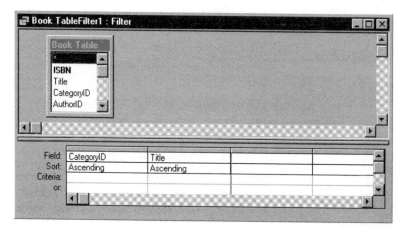

5. Return to the upper pane and double click on the field required for your second level sort – *Title* in our case. In the lower pane set the sort order to **Ascending**

6. Once you have set up the options required, click the **Apply Filter** tool ▽ to display your records in the new order

ISBN	Title	Category	AuthorID	Publishe
▶ 0 45 469861 2	Hamsters at Home	Animals	8	
0 587 39561 0	Changing Skys	Astronomy	16	
0 576 26111 2	Crazy Comets	Astronomy	15	
0 55345 456 2	The Night Sky	Astronomy	2	
0 14 037022 5	Castaways	Children's Fiction	8	
0 14 032382 3	In & Out Stories	Children's Fiction	8	
0 99988 452 1	The Tortoise in the Corner	Children's Fiction	4	
0 412 46512 1	Bits & Bytes	Computing	13	
0 482 31456 1	Easy Internet	Computing	17	
0 15 056473 6	Teach Yourself Access 7	Computing	13	
0 563 49124 5	Bread and Biscuits	Cooking	11	
0 345 12342 3	Campfire Cooking	Cooking	20	
0 758 34512 1	Perfect Pizzas	Cooking	11	
0 664 58123 4	Reading with the Under 5's	Education	8	

Record: ◄◄ ◄ 1 ► ►► ►* of 20

Saving sorted records separately

If you do not want to overwrite the original record order, but you want to save the sort options you have set up for future use, you can save the options as a Query. You must return to the Filter dialog box to do this (**Records, Filter, Advanced Filter/Sort...**).

● Click the **Save** tool on the toolbar within the **Filter** dialog box. Give your query a suitable name – *Sorted on Category then Title* – and click **OK**.

Your query will be listed on the **Queries** tab in the **Database** window.

Your filter criteria have been saved as a Query. When you open the query from the **Database** window, it appears in a **Select Query** window, rather than the **Filter** window in which it was designed.

8.4 Find

To locate a record in your table, you can use the record selector buttons at the bottom of your datasheet or form, or go to a specific record number by specifying the record number in the number field within the record selector buttons and pressing [Enter].

If you have a lot of records in your table, the Find function can provide a quick way of locating a specific record.

Try locating a book in a particular category:

1. Place the insertion point anywhere within the *Category* field in the *Book* table

2. Click the **Find** tool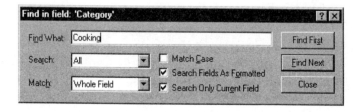

3. At the **Find** dialog box, enter the detail you are looking for – *Cooking* in this example

4. Edit the other fields as necessary – as *Category* looks up its values in the *Category* table, you must select the **Search Fields As Formatted** checkbox

5. Click **Find First** to find the first occurrence that matches your find string

6. If it is not the record you want, click **Find Next** until you reach the record you are looking for

7. Close the dialog box once you have found your record

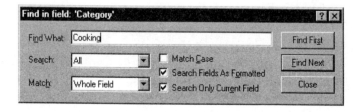

—————————— **8.5 Filter** ——————————

There will be times when you want to display a specific group of records from your table – a list of American authors, or authors who specialise in travel books for example.

This is done by *filtering* the records. You can filter your records **By Selection** or **By Form**.

Filter By Selection

Try filtering the *Author* table to display those of a specific nationality.

1. Open the *Author* table

2. Position the insertion point in the field of a record that has the criteria you are looking for – if you are looking for American authors, position the insertion field within the *Nationality* field, in a record where the author is American

3. Click the **Filter By Selection** tool

A subset of the records within your table will be displayed.

4. You can filter your filtered list using the same technique – narrowing down your list of records as you go

5. To display all your records again, click the **Remove Filter** tool

Filter By Form

When you **Filter By Form**, you can specify multiple criteria at the one time (unlike **Filter By Selection** where you narrow down your search one criterion at a time).

In our *Author* table we could look for Scottish authors who specialise in Travel.

1. Click the **Filter By Form** tool 🔳

   You are presented with an empty record

   As you move from field to field, you will notice that each field behaves like a Combo Box in which you can display a list of options to choose from.

2. In the *Nationality* field, choose **Scottish** from the list, and in the *Speciality* field choose **Travel** from the list

3. Click the **Apply Filter** tool 🔳 – all records meeting the criteria specified will be displayed

4. You can display all your records again by clicking **Remove Filter** 🔳

—— 8.6 Querying more than one table ——

In the examples up until now, we have sorted and filtered records within one table. There will be times when you need to collect the data you require from several tables, and sort or filter that data.

When working across several tables, you must set up a Query from the Database window.

We will set up a Query to display *Book Title, Author, Publisher* and *Year Published* data.

If you have a table open, close it and return to the **Database** window.

1. At the **Database** window, select the **Queries** tab and click **New**

2. At the **New Query** dialog box, choose **Design View** and click **OK**

3. You will arrive at the **Select Query** dialog box. The **Show**

Table window should be open, listing the tables in your database

(If the **Show Table** window is not open, click the **Show Table** tool 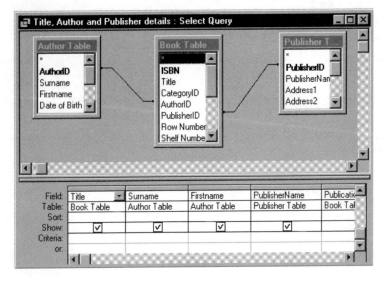 to display the table list)

4. Add the *Author* table, *Book* table and *Publisher* table to the **Select Query** dialog box

5. Close the **Show Table** window

6. You will notice some extra rows in the lower pane of the **Select Query** window

    ◆ The **Table** row displays the name of the table from which a field is taken

    ◆ The **Show** row indicates whether or not a selected field will be displayed in the result – a tick in the box means the field detail will be displayed, no tick means the detail will not be displayed. The default for all fields is that the detail will be displayed

7. Select the fields you want, in the order you want them to appear, from the tables displayed

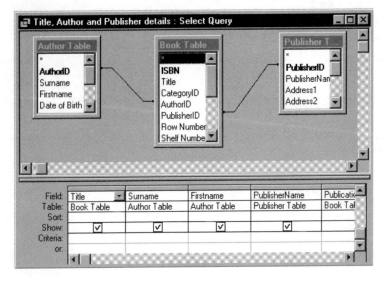

You will need the:

◆ *Title* from the *Book* table

◆ *Surname* and *Firstname* from the *Author* table

◆ *PublisherName* from the *Publisher* table

◆ *Publication year* from the *Book* table

8. Run your query – click the **Run** tool ![] – and note the results

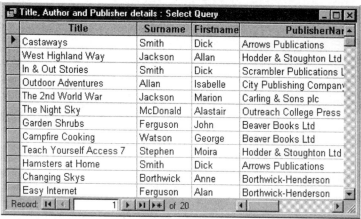

Title	Surname	Firstname	PublisherNar
Castaways	Smith	Dick	Arrows Publications
West Highland Way	Jackson	Allan	Hodder & Stoughton Ltd
In & Out Stories	Smith	Dick	Scrambler Publications L
Outdoor Adventures	Allan	Isabelle	City Publishing Compan
The 2nd World War	Jackson	Marion	Carling & Sons plc
The Night Sky	McDonald	Alastair	Outreach College Press
Garden Shrubs	Ferguson	John	Beaver Books Ltd
Campfire Cooking	Watson	George	Beaver Books Ltd
Teach Yourself Access 7	Stephen	Moira	Hodder & Stoughton Ltd
Hamsters at Home	Smith	Dick	Arrows Publications
Changing Skys	Borthwick	Anne	Borthwick-Henderson
Easy Internet	Ferguson	Alan	Borthwick-Henderson

Record: ◄◄ ◄ 1 ► ►► ►* of 20

The selected fields from *all* your records are displayed.

9. Save your query – you could call it something like, *Title, Author and Publisher details*

10. Close your Query – you will find it on the **Queries** tab in the **Database** window

As you try out the following examples, save any queries you want to keep.

8.7 The Select Query dialog box

If you want a subset of your records, you must specify any criteria you want to base your selected records on in the **Select Query** dialog box. The criteria are specified through expressions that you key into the criteria rows. When entering expressions there are one or two rules you should keep in mind.

If you want to look for multiple criteria being met within the same record, the criteria are entered on the same criteria row. If you wanted a list of all the books published by Hodder & Stoughton Ltd, you would enter **Hodder & Stoughton Ltd** in the *PublisherName* column in the criteria row.

However, if you wanted a list of all the books published by Hodder & Stoughton Ltd in 1992, you would enter **Hodder & Stoughton Ltd** in the *PublisherName* column and **1992** in the *Publication Year* column on the same criteria row.

When you enter criteria in different cells in the same criteria row, Access uses the **And** operator. It looks for all the conditions being met before returning the record details. If you enter criteria in different cells in different criteria rows, Access uses the **Or** operator.

Experiment with different criteria using your tables.

1. Create a new Query in Design View

2. Add the *Book*, *Author* and *Publisher* tables to the **Select Query** window

3. Select the fields you want, in the order you want them to appear – you can use the same ones as in the previous example:

   ◆ *Title* from the *Book* table

   ◆ *Surname* and *Firstname* from the *Author* table

   ◆ *PublisherName* from the *Publisher* table

   ◆ *Publication Year* from the *Book* table

8.8 Or conditions

This time, we want our books in ascending order on the Title field, but we only want to show the books we have from the publishers Hodder & Stoughton Ltd and those from Borthwick-Henderson Ltd. We have also decided not to display the details in the Publication year column.

1. Set the sort order required in the Title column

2. In the *PublisherName* column, enter **Hodder & Stoughton Ltd** in the first criteria row and **Borthwick-Henderson Ltd** in the next criteria row – Access will return records that have **Hodder & Stoughton Ltd** OR **Borthwick-Henderson Ltd** in the *PublisherName* field.

3. Deselect the **Show** checkbox in the *Publication Year* column as we do not want this column displayed in the result

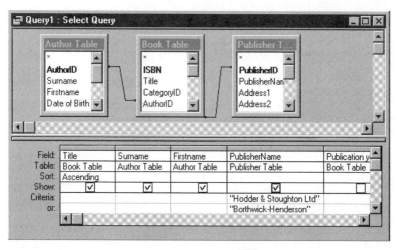

4. Run your query – click the **Run** tool – and note the results

The book titles should be in ascending order, the author name and publisher name are displayed – but only for the publishers specified in the criteria rows. The year of publication is not displayed.

Query1 : Select Query			
Title	**Surname**	**Firstname**	**PublisherName**
African Drums	MacDonald	Donald	Hodder & Stoughton Ltd
Bits & Bytes	Stephen	Moira	Borthwick-Henderson
Changing Skys	Borthwick	Anne	Borthwick-Henderson
Easy Internet	Ferguson	Alan	Borthwick-Henderson
Reading with the Under 5's	Smith	Dick	Hodder & Stoughton Ltd
Teach Yourself Access 7	Stephen	Moira	Hodder & Stoughton Ltd
West Highland Way	Jackson	Allan	Hodder & Stoughton Ltd

Record: 1 of 7

8.9 And conditions

This time try to get a list of all the books published by Hodder &
Stoughton Ltd in 1992.

1. Enter **Hodder & Stoughton Ltd** in the *PublisherName* column
   and **1992** in the *Publication Year* column of the first criteria
   row

2. Run your query – click the Run tool

Access will return details for records where both criteria are met
in the same record – it will return details of records that have
Hodder & Stoughton Ltd in the *PublisherName* field AND **1992**
in the *Publication Year* column.

8.10 Range

You can also set up queries to return records within a specific
range. If you want to specify a range of values, use the operators:

<, >, <=, >=, =, <>

or

Between...And...

in your expressions.

To get a list of books by authors whose surname began with the letter **M** through to the end of the alphabet, you would enter **>M** in the criteria row of the *Surname* column.

If you want a list of books published before 1994, you would enter **<1994** in the criteria row in the *Publication Year* column.

To get a list of all the books published in 1992, 1993, 1994, 1995 and 1996 you would enter **Between 1992 And 1996** in the criteria row of the *Publication Year* column.

The on-line help will give you other examples of expressions you can experiment with.

—————— 8.11 Prompt for input ——————

There may be times when you run the same query regularly, but you need to change the criteria each time. Instead of entering the criteria into the Design view for the query, you can enter a ***prompt*** that will appear on the screen requesting your input each time you run the query.

You could set up a query that will list the books written by a specific author with a prompt to ask you for the author name each time the query is run.

1. In the criteria row, in the *Surname* column enter the prompt you wish to appear on the screen when the query is run:

[Enter Surname]

2. Enter a similar prompt in the *Firstname* column:

[Enter Firstname]

The prompts ***must*** be included within **[square brackets]**, and they ***cannot*** consist of just the field name, although the field name may be included within the prompt – **[Surname]** won't work, but **[Enter Surname]** will!

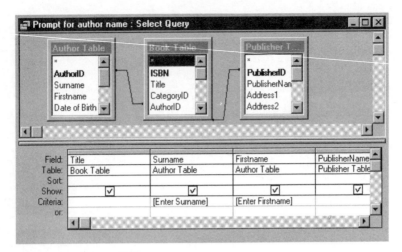

3. Run the query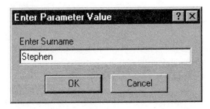

4. Enter the *Surname* detail, and click **OK**

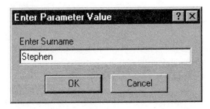

5. Enter the *Firstname* detail, and click **OK**

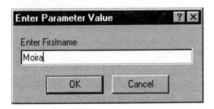

The results will be displayed on your screen.

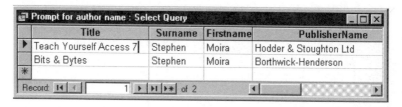

6. Save this Query – you could call it *Prompt for author name*

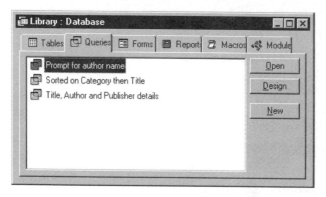

You will find the queries you have saved on the **Queries** tab in the **Database** window.

● To run a query from the **Database** window, double click on the query name, or select the query and click **Open**.

● To display the **Select Query** window for a query, select the query and click **Design**.

———— 8.12 Chapter summary ————

In this chapter you have learnt how to sort the data in your tables and extract records that meet specific criteria.

You have learnt how to:

● Perform a simple sort.

● Perform a multi-level sort.

● Find records.

● Filter data by selection.

● Filter data by form.

● Extract data from several tables.

●· Create expressions to display details of records that meet specific criteria.

9

REPORTS

9.1 Aims of this chapter

Reports provide an effective way of producing a printed copy of the data extracted or calculated from your tables and queries.

In this chapter you will be introduced to some of the methods you can use to generate reports. You will learn how to produce reports using AutoReport, by manually designing a report and by using a Report Wizard to generate labels.

9.2 AutoReport

You can quickly design a simple report from any of your tables or queries using the AutoReport object. The report produced is a simple, single column report, listing all the fields in each record of the table or query.

You can create an AutoReport from a table or query that is open, or from the **Database** window.

To create an AutoReport from an open table or query

1. Display the **New Object** list

2. Select **AutoReport**

A simple report will be created using the data in the table or query you have open.

3. When you close your report you will be asked if you want to save it. If you save it, the report will be listed on the **Reports** tab in the **Database** window

You do not need to open a table or query before you can generate an AutoReport from it – you can do so from the **Database** window.

The report below was based on the *Title, Author and Publisher details* query set up in Chapter 8.

To generate an AutoReport from the Database window

1. Select the table or query you want to base your report on (*Title, Author and Publisher details* query in this example)

2. Choose **AutoReport** from the **New Object** list

Reports are displayed in Print Preview – so you can see what your page would look like if you were to print it out.

You can use the Page arrows at the bottom of the Print Preview window to move through the pages in your report.

On this report, the detail from six records fits on each page – this will obviously vary from report to report as the amount of detail in some tables and queries will be considerably more than in others.

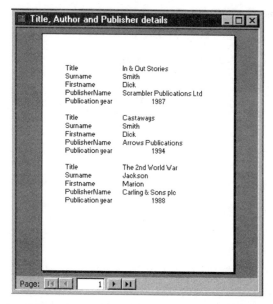

3. Click the **Close** tool on the Print Preview toolbar to take your report through into Design view

The Design view of a report looks very similar to the Design view of a form – many of the design features discussed in Chapter 7 on Forms Design are also used in report design.

The main areas in a report are the:

● **Detail** area

● **Page Header and Footer** area

● **Report Header and Footer** area

The Page Header and Footer areas are displayed by default in an AutoReport design, and you can enter anything you want to appear at the top or bottom of each page of your report in these areas.

The Field List, containing the field names from the table or query on which the report is based, is displayed – you can toggle the display of this by clicking the Field List tool 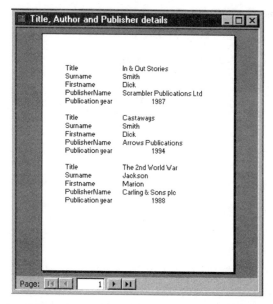.

——— 9.3 Page Header and Footer ———

Page Headers are often used for column headings, or the report title; Page Footers are usually used for page numbering.

Adding a Page Header

You can easily add a Page Header using the **Label** tool. You used the **Label** tool in Form design to add headings, instructions and other text to your form. The same techniques are used in Report design. Add the page header – **Books held in the library**

1. Click the **Label** tool [A]

2. Move the mouse pointer into the **Page Header** area – the mouse pointer becomes an ⁺**A** shape

3. Click and drag to draw a rectangle to indicate the position of the text you are going to key in

4. When you let go the mouse, the insertion point is within the area you have outlined

5. Type in your header text – **Books held in the library**

6. Click outside your heading when you have finished

Format the heading:

7. Select the label (click on it once)

8. Use the tools on the formatting toolbar to increase the font size, change its colour, make it bold, etc.

Adding a Page Footer

In the page footer area of a report, the page number is usually shown. The page number is placed in a **Text Box**.

1. If necessary, scroll down through your form until you see the **Page Footer** area

2. Click the Text Box tool [abl] then click and drag in the **Page Footer** area to indicate the position of the Text Box

A **Text Box** field consists of a description (the left part) and a detail area (the right part)

3. Delete the description (left) part of the text box – select it and press the [Delete] key on your keyboard

To get Access to put a page number in the Text Box:

4. Select the box – click on it once

5. Click the **Properties** tool ![icon] to open the dialog box displaying the properties for this object

6. On the **Data** tab, enter **=[Page]** in the **Control Source** field

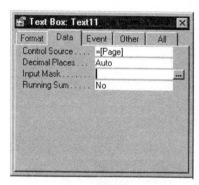

7. Close the dialog box

Your design screen should be similar to the one shown here.

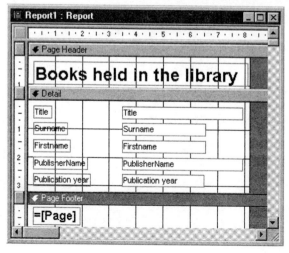

——9.4 Save, print preview and print——

1. Click the **Save** tool on the toolbar to save your report

2. At the **Save As** dialog box, give your report a suitable name

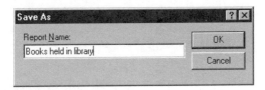

3. Click **OK**

4. Take your form through into Print Preview to see how it looks now – note the Page Header and Footer that you have set up on each page

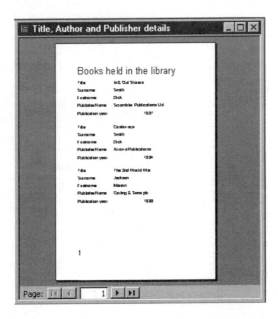

With reports created using AutoReport the title bar of the report in Print Preview displays the name of the table or query on which your report is based – not the name that you saved your report under.

5. To print your report out, click the **Print** tool  on the **Print Preview** toolbar

6. Close your Report to return to the **Database** window – click ⊠ on the right of the **Print Preview** title bar

Your report will be listed on the Reports tab of the Database window.

Once you have set a report up and saved it, you can print it from the **Database** window without previewing it. Select the report you want to print from the **Reports** tab and click the **Print** tool on the **Database** toolbar.

9.5 Report design

You can design your own report layout, arranging the fields as you want them to appear on the design grid.

In this example, we will design a report that will display details of the title, author and publisher of our books, but the detail will be grouped on publisher – so all the books from each publisher will be listed together.

We will base this report on the *Title, Author and Publisher details* query.

1. Click **New** on the **Reports** tab in the **Database** window

2. At the **New Report** dialog box, select **Design View** and choose the table or query from which the data will come – *Title, Author and Publisher details*

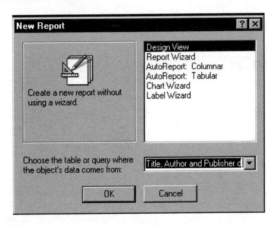

3. Click **OK**

At the design grid, set up the Detail area to display the *Book Title, Author* and *Publication Year* data.

4. Drag the fields you require from the field list into the Detail area

5. Delete the description part of each field (we will add column headings later) and line up the Detail area as required – I suggest in a single row across your grid

6. Decrease the size of the Detail area so that it will produce a neat list – drag the bottom border of the Detail area up – until it looks similar to the illustration below

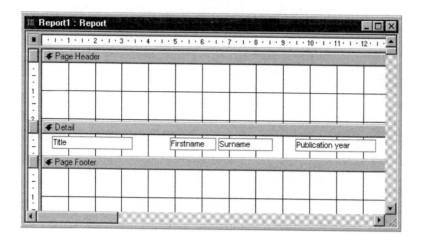

9.6 Layout preview

As you are designing your report, you can preview it whenever you want to check how things are going.

If you are working with a table or query that has a lot of data in it, doing a Print Preview each time you want to check things out may prove a bit time consuming as Access prepares a preview of *all* of the data in your table or query. To speed things up a bit choose **Layout Preview** from the view options instead. Access will prepare two pages of data – which is enough to let you check the layout.

If you want, you can do a Print Preview before you send your report to the printer, to check that every page is as it should be.

9.7 Grouping

On this report, we want to group the books so that all the books from each Publisher are listed together.

This is set up in the **Sorting and Grouping** dialog box.

1. Click the **Sorting and Grouping** tool ▣ to open the dialog box

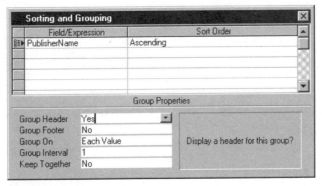

2. Set the **Field/Expression** field to *PublisherName* – select the field from the drop down list

3. Set the **Sort Order** to **Ascending** – so the publisher groups will be in alphabetical order

4. In the **Group Properties** pane set the **Group Header** property to **Yes** – we want a header at the beginning of each group to display the publisher name

5. Close the dialog box to return to your design grid

6. Drag the *PublisherName* field from the **Field List** into the *PublisherName Header* area on your grid

7. Format it as required – as it is a heading, you might want to format it with a larger font, or bold, or both

8. Use the **Label** tool to put column headings inside the *PublisherName Header* area – these could be *Title, Author* and *Year Published*. Format them as required

Your report design should now be similar to this illustration.

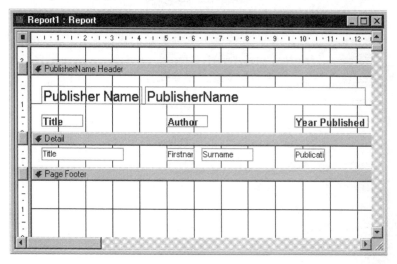

9. In the **Page Header** area, insert an appropriate heading for each page – **Current Book Stock**

10. Number the pages in the **Page Footer** area – insert a **Text Box**, and delete the description (left) part

If you want the footer to say **Page 1**, **Page 2** etc rather than simply **1, 2** you need to enter **="Page " & [Page]** in the **Control Source** field on the **Data** tab of the **Properties** dialog box for the field.

——— 9.8 Report Header and Footer ———

A Report Header goes at the beginning of your report (at the beginning of the first page), a Report Footer goes at the end of it (at the end of the last page).

The Header is often used to describe the contents of the report; the Footer to identify the author and the date the report was printed.

1. To add a Report Header and Footer section, choose **Report Header/Footer** from the **View** menu

2. In the **Report Header** area, use the **Label** tool to insert a field for your report header. Key in your header – **Book List Grouped Under Publisher Headings** – and format it as required

3. In the **Report Footer** area, insert a **Label** field and enter your name

We also want to insert the date in the report footer.

4. Insert a **Text Box** and delete the description part

5. Select the **Detail** part and open the dialog box displaying the properties for the field – click the **Properties** tool 🔳

6. Enter the **Control Source** as **= Date()** – this will produce the current date in the format 19/12/96

9.9 Finishing touches

By using the Toolbox and the Formatting toolbar, you can add the finishing touches to the objects in your report (or form) by adding lines, borders, colour and special effects.

We could add a border to the Publisher Group heading and format the border using the options available.

To add a border

1. Click the **Rectangle** tool 🔳 on the Toolbox

2. Click and drag over the *Publisher Header* area – to draw a border around the label and detail parts

When you let go the mouse button, the label and detail area are hidden. This is because they are under the rectangle you have just drawn. You must send the rectangle behind the text you want to show.

3. Select the rectangle if you have deselected it

4. Open the **Format** menu

5. Choose **Send to Back**

The rectangle is sent behind the label and detail area and your label and detail area should be visible.

If you want a top and bottom border only, use the **Line** tool instead of the **Rectangle** tool. Click and drag to draw your lines wherever you want them.

You can change the line colour, thickness and add other effects to your border.

Select the rectangle and experiment with the following tools to create different effects:

6. Change the border colour using the **Border Colour** tool

7. Make the border thicker or thinner using the **Border Width** tool

8. Select a different background colour using the **Back Colour** tool

9. Create a special effect using the **Special Effect** tool

Use the **Line** tool to draw a line above and below your report heading. Experiment with the formatting on it until you get an effect you like.

10. Save your report under *Books grouped by Publisher*

11. Preview your report and print it if you wish

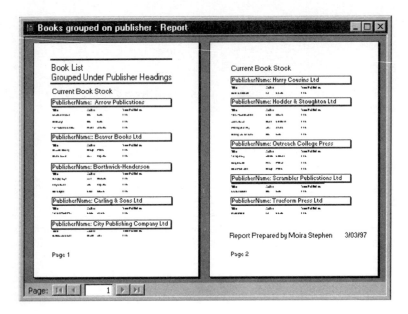

Books grouped on publisher : Report

Book List
Grouped Under Publisher Headings

Current Book Stock

PublisherName: Arrow Publications

PublisherName:: Beaver Books Ltd

PublisherName: Borthwick-Henderson

PublisherName: Carling & Sons Ltd

PublisherName: City Publishing Company Ltd

Page 1

Current Book Stock

PublisherName: Harry Cousins Ltd

PublisherName: Hodder & Stoughton Ltd

PublisherName: Outreach College Press

PublisherName: Scrambler Publications Ltd

PublisherName: Trueform Press Ltd

Report Prepared by Moira Stephen   3/03/97

Page 2

Page: 1

12. Close your report when you've finished – it will be listed on the **Reports** tab in the **Database** window

9.10 Labels

If any of your tables contain names and addresses, you will most probably need to prepare labels from them from time to time. Labels are very easily prepared in Access using the Label Wizard.

In this example, we will go through the steps required to produce labels for the publishers we have in our Publisher table.

1. On the Reports tab in the **Database** window, click **New**

2. At the **New Report** dialog box, choose **Label Wizard** from the list and select the *Publisher* table as the table on which the report is based. Click **OK**

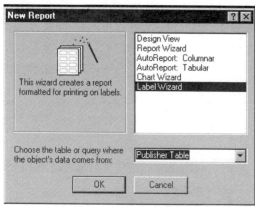

There are about 75 different Avery label specifications set up in the wizard ready for you to use (if you don't use Avery labels, click the Customize button to set up your own label specification).

3. Select the label size required and click **Next**. Select the font and font attributes you wish to use and click **Next**

4. Select the fields required for your label from the **Available fields** list and add them to the **Prototype Label** layout

5. Press [Enter] each time a new line is needed

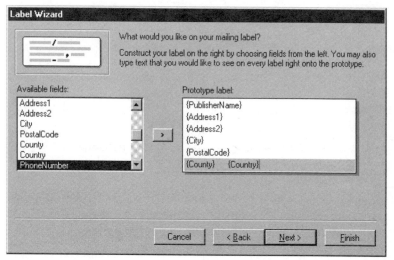

If you add a field by mistake, you can select it in the **Prototype Label** and delete it by pressing [Delete] on your keyboard.

6. At the next step, specify the sort field (or fields) if required. If you want the labels printed in publisher name order, add *PublisherName* to the **Sort by** list

7. At the checkered flag, edit the report name if necessary (the default name is usually okay), choose **See the labels as they will look printed** and click **Finish**

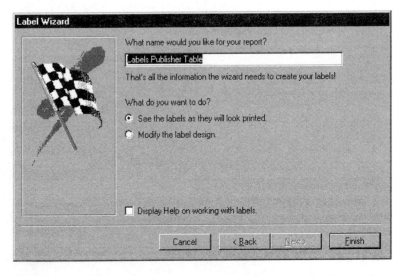

A Print Preview of the labels will appear on your screen. If you don't like the labels, you can take them into Design view and change the font or font attributes, or you could work through the wizard again specifying different criteria.

8. If you want to print your labels, load your label stationery into your printer then click the **Print** tool on the **Print Preview** toolbar

When you close your report, you will find it listed on the Reports tab in the Database window. If you need to print the same set of labels again, you can easily do so without having to set the whole thing up.

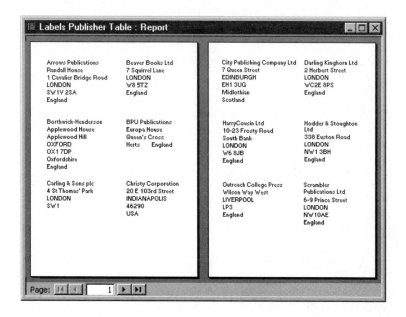

9.11 Chapter summary

In this chapter we have discussed reports, and looked at some of the ways you can use them to produce printed output from your tables and queries. You have learnt how to:

● Set up a simple report using AutoReport.

● Design a report from scratch.

● Group records within a report.

● Add page numbers to your pages.

● Print the current date on your report.

● Add lines and borders.

● Create labels.

● Print your reports.

10

DATABASE WIZARD

10.1 Aims of this chapter

In this chapter we will look at a quick and easy alternative to setting up our database from scratch. In this chapter we will use a wizard to automate the process of setting up our database, rather than use the Blank database as we did in the Library example.

You should close the Library database if it is open, as we are going to create a new database using one of the wizards provided.

10.2 Database Wizards

Access 7 comes complete with a set of over 20 database wizards that automate the process of setting up a database. The wizards include things like Wine List, Music Collection, Order Entry, Students and Classes, Recipes – they are quite varied and worth looking at, as they may save you a lot of setting up time.

1. Click the **New** tool on the **Database** toolbar

2. At the **New** dialog box, select the **Databases** tab

3. Select the Database Wizard you want to use – choose **Membership**

4. Click **OK**

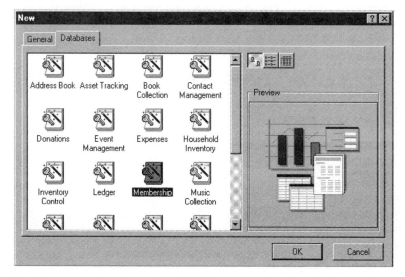

5. Give your database a suitable name – *Car Club Membership* in my case

6. Click **Create**

The first wizard screen will give you a list of what will be stored in the database, in this case:

◆ Information about members

◆ Types of membership available

◆ Information about committees

◆ Payment information

◆ Information about my organisation

7. Click Next to move onto the next step

You are presented with the list of tables that will be included in your database down the left hand side of the dialog box.

If you select a table on the left side, a list of the fields that will be set up in that table are displayed down the right side.

If you look through the list of fields for any table, you will find most of the field names have a tick beside them – they are selected for inclusion in the table.

8. Look through the tables and select and deselect fields as required. The *Information about members* table has some deselected fields in it that you might want to use

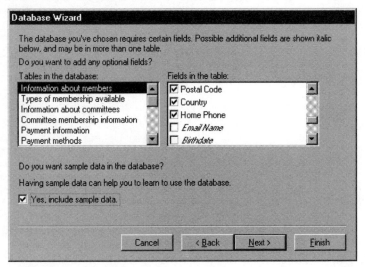

9. Select the checkbox to include **sample data** in your database

Sample data is useful – you can experiment and practise on the data until you see how the database works. I'd recommend you include sample data the first time you set up a database using any wizard.

10. At the next step, choose a style for the screen displays in your database

11. Select the style you want to use for the reports you will be printing

12. Enter your database title at the next step, e.g. **Car Club Membership**

13. If you want a picture on your reports, select the **Yes, I'd like to include a picture** checkbox, then click the **Picture...** button and choose the picture to include (you'll find lots in the ClipArt folder within the MS Office folder to choose from)

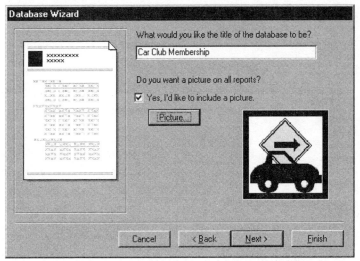

14. When you click **Next**, you will be at the checkered flag. If you want help on using the database, select the **Display Help on using a Database** checkbox (if you've worked through the book this far, you shouldn't need to display any help)

15. Click **Finish**

—— 10.3 Exploring your database ——

Access will spend a little time building your database, and when it has finished, the database will be open on your screen, ready for use. The **Database** window for your database is minimised (you can see it at the bottom left of your screen).

The **Main Switchboard** for your database is displayed. This is an alternative to the **Database** window and is perhaps more user

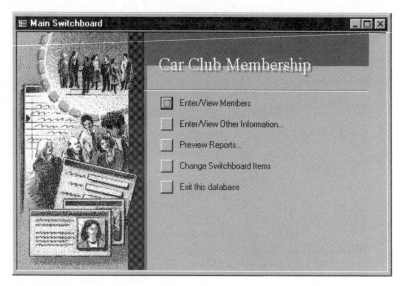

friendly. You use the Switchboard to navigate through your forms and reports, and to enter and update data in the tables.

10.4 Enter/View Members

This option displays the *Members* form. It is made up of text boxes, combo boxes, checkboxes, and so on, which we discussed when setting up the *Library* forms in Chapter 7.

The *Members* form contains a lot of information and runs to two pages. Rather than scroll through the form, it has been set up as two pages, which you can move between using the Page buttons.

You can add new members, delete existing members or edit the detail on any member from this form.

In addition to the detail fields, there are buttons which take you through to other forms in your database.

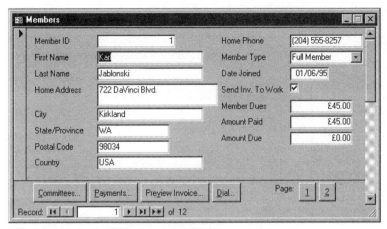

Other forms in the Members database

The **Committees...** button takes you through to the *Member Committees* form (this form has a subform within it).

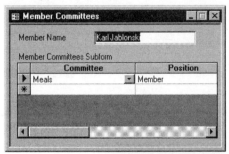

The **Payments...** button takes you through to the *Payments* form.

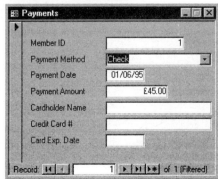

The **Preview Invoice...** button takes you through to the *Print Invoice* form.

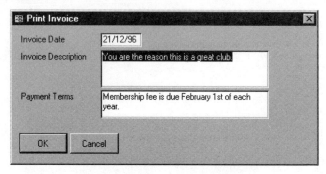

The **Dial...** button takes you through to the *AutoDialer* form.

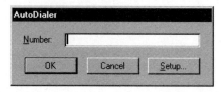

— 10.5 Enter/View Other Information —

This option takes you through to the **Forms Switchboard** which lists the forms that will display the other information in your database. The forms display details on:

● Committees

● Member Types

● Payment Methods

● Your Organisation

The forms have been designed using the techniques discussed in Chapter 7. They contain text boxes, checkboxes and subforms.

You can edit the design of any of these forms by taking them into Design view.

● When you have finished exploring the forms, return to the Main Switchboard.

10.6 Preview Reports

Several reports have been set up by the wizard. These are listed in the Reports Switchboard.

● Invoice Report (this has actually been set up as a form)

● Alphabetical Member Listing Report

● Committee Members Report

● Listing by Membership Type Report

● Outstanding Balances Report

If you opted to display a picture on your reports, you will notice the picture on the reports you preview.

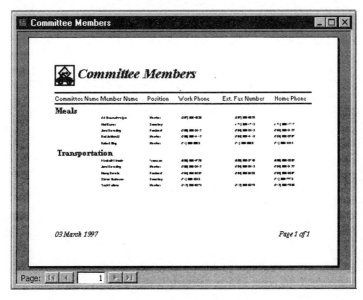

Some of the reports are simple lists, others have the contents grouped into categories, e.g. Committee Members.

Notice the **Page Header/Footer** sections in this report. The **Page Header** contains the column headings and the **Page Footer** contains the current date and page number.

● Return to the **Main Switchboard** when you have finished previewing your reports.

—— 10.7 Change Switchboard items ——

This option lets you edit the Switchboards that have been set up for the database. You can change the default Switchboard (the Main Switchboard in this database), add new items to Switchboards, edit existing items, and delete items from Switchboards.

We will set up our own Switchboards in Chapter 11 and work with this feature.

—————— 10.8 Exit this database ——————

This option closes the database.

—— 10.9 Closing the Switchboard ——

If you close a Switchboard by clicking its close button ⊠, the database remains open; you've simply closed the Switchboard 'user interface' to it. The Switchboard is a form, listed on the **Forms** tab of the **Database** window. You can open the Switchboard again by opening the Switchboard form.

10.10 Database window

You may have noticed the **Database** window minimised at the bottom left of your screen.

If you restore the **Database** window, you will find the tables, queries, forms and reports listed on the tabs within the **Database** window as usual.

You can check out the design of any of the tables, queries, forms or reports and edit them if you wish.

WARNING

Do not edit the Switchboard form in **Form Design** View - you may find your application no longer works!

10.11 Chapter summary

This chapter has introduced you to the database wizards. Database wizards automate the process of setting up a database and can save you a lot of time – as long as you can find one that is useful to you! You have learnt how to:

● Create a new database using a wizard.

● Navigate your way through your database using the Switchboards.

● Explore the forms and reports within your database via a Switchboard.

● Display the Database window of the database created using a wizard.

11

SWITCHBOARDS

11.1 Aims of this chapter

In Chapter 10 we set up a database using a wizard. The wizard created Switchboards that could be used to help you navigate your way through your forms and reports. In this chapter you will learn how to set up a Switchboard for your *Library* database. Switchboards offer you a user friendly front end to your database. They are particularly useful if you are setting up the database for a relatively inexperienced Access user.

11.2 Creating the Main Switchboard

You can create a Switchboard for any database you build. It is often easier to navigate your way through a database using a Switchboard. If you are designing a database for someone else to use, a Switchboard will distance them from the tables and design code to a considerable extent.

To create a Switchboard, the database you want to create a Switchboard for must be open.

1. Open your *Library* database if it isn't already open

2. Choose **Add Ins** from the **Tools** menu

3. Pick **Switchboard Manager** from the list

4. If you are prompted to create a Switchboard, click **Yes**

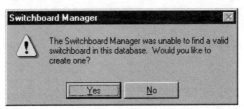

Access will create a Switchboard Items table on the Tables tab in the Database window and a Switchboard form on the Forms tab.

The **Switchboard Manager** dialog box will appear, with the Main Switchboard listed on it. From here, you can add items to the main Switchboard and create other Switchboards.

The first thing you need to do is decide where you want to be able to go to from the Main Switchboard. Is it to other Switchboards or directly into a form or report? In most cases it is probably a mixture of both.

In this example we need to set up two more Switchboards that can be accessed from the Main Switchboard – one to list most of our forms and one for our reports.

— 11.3 Creating extra Switchboards —

1. Click the **New...** button

2. Enter a name for your Switchboard

3. Click **OK**

You could call the form *Switchboard Edit/View Forms* and the report *Switchboard Preview Reports*.

–11.4 Adding to the Main Switchboard–

You must now add the items you want to appear on the Main Switchboard. Here are three such items.

Item 1

In this example, we want first to list an option to take us to the **Edit/View Forms Switchboard** and then one to take us to the **Preview Reports Switchboard**.

1. Select the **Main Switchboard** at the **Switchboard Manager** dialog box

2. Click the **Edit...** button

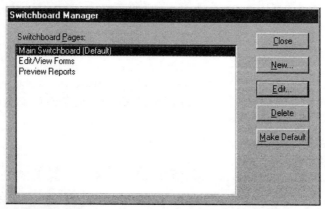

This takes you through to a dialog box where you can set up the items you wish to appear on your Main Switchboard.

3. At the **Edit Switchboard Page** dialog box, click **New...** to add a new item to the Switchboard

   At the **Edit Switchboard Item** dialog box:

4. Enter the text you want to appear on the Main Switchboard page, e.g. **Enter/View other information**

5. Pick the appropriate command from the command list (**Go to Switchboard** for this one)

6. Select the Switchboard you want this option to take you to in the Switchboard field, e.g. **Edit/View Forms**

7. Click **OK**

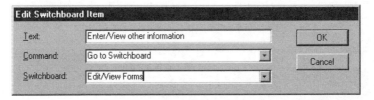

8. Now do the same for the **Preview Reports Switchboard**

This time the text that will appear on your main Switchboard could be **Preview Reports**, the Command would be **Go to Switchboard** and the Switchboard would be **Preview Reports** (if that was what you called this Switchboard).

Item 2

We also want to add an option to the Main Switchboard to take us through to the *Books, Authors and Publishers form* as this is the one we use most often.

1. From the **Edit Switchboard** dialog box, click **New...**

2. In the **Text** field, enter the text you want to appear on the Main Switchboard, e.g. **Book details**

3. In the **Command** field, choose **Open Form in Edit Mode**

4. In the **Form** field choose *Book, Author and Publisher details*

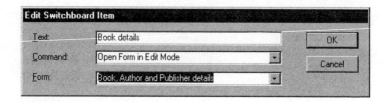

5. Click **OK**

Item 3

Finally, we need to add an option to close the database.

1. From the **Edit Switchboard Page** dialog box, click **New...**

2. In the **Text** field, enter the text you want to appear on the Main Switchboard, e.g. **Close Database**

3. In the **Command** field, choose **Exit Application**

4. Click **OK**

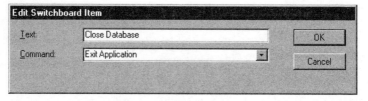

You have now successfully set up the options required on your Main Switchboard.

At the **Edit Switchboard Page**, check the order of the options you have listed. The option most often used should be at the top of the list – *Book details* in our case.

1. To move *Book details* up to the top of the list, select it and click the **Move Up** button until it is in position

2. Close the **Edit Switchboard Page** dialog box

—— 11.5 Adding to other Switchboards ——

This is done in the same way as setting up the Main Switchboard.

The Edit/View Forms Switchboard

In the *Edit/View Forms* Switchboard, you will need to set up an option for each form you wish to view.

You will also need to set up an option to return you to the Main Switchboard.

1. Select the *Edit/View Forms* Switchboard in the **Switchboard Manager** dialog box

2. Click **Edit...**

3. Add the items required to the *Edit/View Forms* Switchboard, e.g. the forms you have already created and are on the **Forms** tab of your *Library* database

To add the Publisher detail form

1. Click **New...** at the **Edit Switchboard Page** dialog box

2. Enter the text you want to appear listed on your *Edit/View Forms* Switchboard, e.g. **Publisher names and addresses**

3. Choose **Open Form in Edit Mode** in the **Command** field

4. Select the *Publisher detail form* from the list of forms available in the **Form** field

5. Click **OK**

If you have forgotten what forms you have to choose from, and can't think of what to enter into the **Text** field, complete the **Command** field and **Form** field first, then go back to the **Text** field once you know what form you are dealing with.

The items on your *Edit/View Forms* Switchboard should be similar to those illustrated below.

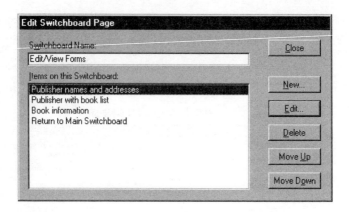

The Preview Reports Switchboard

In the Preview Reports Switchboard, you will need to set up an option for each report you want to preview.

You will also need to set up an option to return you to the Main Switchboard.

1. Select the *Preview Reports* Switchboard in the **Switchboard Manager** dialog box

2. Click **Edit...**

3. Add the items required to the *Preview Reports* Switchboard

To add the Books held in library report

1. Click **New...** at the **Edit Switchboard Page** dialog box

2. Enter the text you want to appear listed on your *Preview Reports* Switchboard, e.g. **Books currently held**

3. Choose **Open Report** in the **Command** field

4. Select the *Books held in library* from the list of reports available in the **Report** field

5. Click **OK**

If you have forgotten what reports you have to choose from, and can't think of what to enter into the **Text** field, complete the **Command** field and **Report** field first, then go back to the **Text** field once you know what report you are dealing with.

Your *Preview Reports* Switchboard should be similar to the one below.

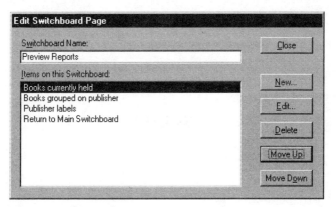

Closing and testing

Now close Switchboard Manager

1. Click **Close** at the **Edit Switchboard Page** dialog box

2. Click **Close** at the **Switchboard Manager** dialog box

Try your new Switchboards out:

1. Open the **Switchboards** form on the **Forms** tab in your **Database** window

2. If the Switchboards don't work as expected go back into Switchboard Manager (Tools, Add Ins, Switchboard Manager) and check the options you have set up

11.6 Adding a picture

In the Switchboards that are created using the Database wizards, a picture is included down the left side of the Switchboard.

You can easily add a picture to your own Switchboards if you wish.

1. Close the Switchboard if necessary and return to the **Database** window

    You will find a Switchboard form listed on your **Forms** tab. To add a picture to this form you must take it into Design View. **Do not** edit anything else on the form.

2. Select your Switchboard form and click **Design**

3. Select the left side of the form under the **Detail** border – click in the space once

    An Image object has been set up here, ready to display the picture of your choice.

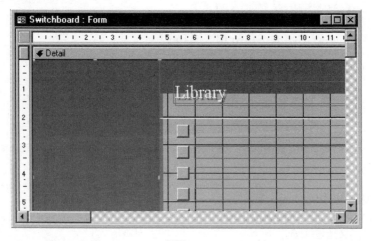

4. Click the **Properties** tool to open the **Image Properties** dialog box

5. Select the **Format** tab or the **All** tab within the **Image Properties** dialog box

6. Locate the **Picture** field – it is at the top of the list on the **Format** tab, or second on the list on the **All** tab

7. Enter the path and filename of the picture you want to use

If you do not know the path or filename, click the **Build** button ▦ to the right of the **Picture** field and navigate through your folders until you have found the picture you want to use. There are lots of pictures in the Clipart folder within MSOffice to choose from.

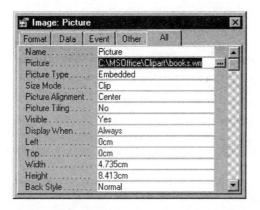

8. Experiment with the **Size Mode** options to get the effect you want from your picture – I thought **Clip** worked best with my choice

9. Close the **Image** dialog box when you have finished

10. Save the changes to your form

11. Return to **Form** view

You should find that the picture is displayed on all of your Switchboards.

—— 11.7 Starting at the Switchboard ——

Once you have set your Switchboard up, you will most often want
to use it as the 'user interface' to your database.

You can get Access to display your Switchboard form
automatically (rather than the Database window) when you open
your database.

1. Open the **Tools** menu and choose **Startup...**

2. Select **Switchboard** from the list of forms available in the
   Display Form field

3. Click **OK**

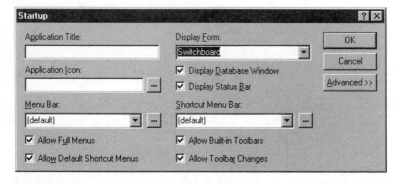

The next time you open your database the Main Switchboard
will appear on your screen.

────── 11.8 Chapter summary ──────

In this chapter you have learnt how to set up a Switchboard for your database.

You have learnt how to:

● Create the Main Switchboard.

● Create additional Switchboards.

● Add items to the Switchboards.

● Include a picture on your Switchboard.

● Display the Switchboard automatically each time you open your database.

12

MACROS and MODULES

12.1 Aims of this chapter

In this chapter we will introduce you to macros and also mention modules. Macros and modules are extremely powerful – this chapter can offer only a glimpse of what is possible. If you wish to become an Access 'guru', perhaps developing applications for less experienced users, you can check out the on-line help to find out more about these objects.

12.2 Introducing macros

In Chapter 10 on Database Wizard we set up a *Car Club Membership* database. From the *Members* form, you could move to the *Committees*, *Payments*, *Preview Invoice* and *Dial* forms by clicking on a button. The buttons had been placed in the **Form Footer** area in **Form Design** view.

We could set up a similar routine when working in our *Library* database.

In our Library database, the main form that we use is the *Book, Author and Publisher* one. If you are viewing the *Book, Author and Publisher* form and discover that you need to view any other form, it can be quite tedious jumping back to the Database window to open another form, or moving and re-sizing windows to fit several forms on the screen at the same time.

A more efficient option is to set up control buttons similar to those in the *Car Club Membership* database within the *Book, Author and Publisher* form, and open the other forms you need to view from within the *Book, Author and Publisher* form.

One way of achieving this is to set up a macro containing the instructions to open the required form, then assign this macro to a control button within the *Book, Author and Publisher* form.

You can use macros for many things. The list below gives only a few examples.

● Open any table, form, query or report in any available view.

● Close any open table, form, query or report.

● Open a report in Print Preview.

● Send a report to the printer.

● Execute any of the commands on the Access menus.

We will set up some very simple macros to add to our *Book, Author and Publisher* form.

——————12.3 Recording a macro——————

Let's say we had decided that we wanted to be able to open our *Publisher detail* form and our *Books grouped on publisher* report from within the *Book, Author and Publisher* form.

The first thing we need to do is record two macros:

● one containing the instructions to open the *Publisher detail* form in Form view

- one containing the instructions to open the *Books grouped on publisher* report in Print Preview.

Recording a macro

- Select the **Macros** tab in the **Database** window and click **New**.

The **Macro Design** view window appears. It is very similar to the Table Design view window with an upper and lower pane.

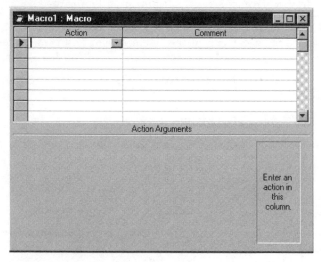

Open the Publisher detail form

We will deal with the *Publisher detail* form first.

1. In the **Action** column, choose **OpenForm** from the drop down list of options

2. Enter a description of what the action will achieve in the **Comments** column. This is optional – it is simply a description of what will happen – you can leave the comment column blank if you wish

3. In the lower pane, in the **Form Name** field, choose *Publisher detail* form from the drop down list

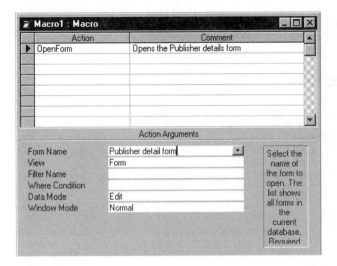

The default settings in the rest of the lower pane are fine.

4. Save your macro. Give it a name that describes what it does – it's easier to remember what a macro does if you name it sensibly

5. Close the **Macro design** view

Your new macro should be listed on the **Macros** tab in the **Database** window.

Open the Books grouped on publisher report

This time you will create a new macro that will open your report in Print Preview.

1. Select **OpenReport** as **Action**

2. The **Report Name** is *Books grouped on publisher*

3. Set the **View** to **Print Preview**

4. Save your Macro – you could call it *Books grouped on publisher*

5. Close your **Macro design** view

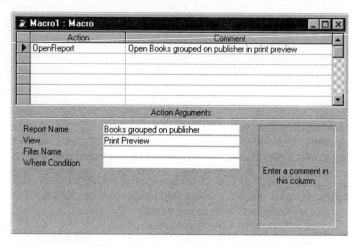

You should have two macros listed on the **Macros** tab in the **Database** window.

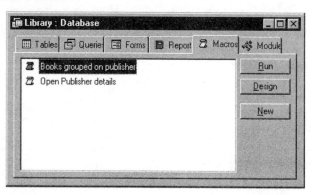

Before going any further, check that your macros work.

12.4 Testing a macro

1. Select **Open Publisher details**

2. Click **Run**

Your publisher detail form should appear on your screen. Close it and test the other macro.

3. Select *Books grouped on publisher*

4. Click **Run**

A preview of the report should appear on the screen.

If either of the macros don't work as expected, select the macro and click **Design** to return to **Design** view. Check through the macro specification and fix your error.

12.5 Assigning a macro to a button

The next task is to assign these macros to control buttons within the *Book, Author and Publisher details* form.

Once this has been done, you will be able to open the *Publisher detail* form and preview the *Books grouped on publisher* report from within the *Book, Author and Publisher details* form.

1. Take the *Book, Author and Publisher details* form into **Design** view

2. Scroll down to view the **Form Footer** area (resize the footer area if necessary)

The easiest way to get the macros onto your form is to drag them from the Database window and drop them into the Form Footer.

3. Click the **Database window** tool to display the **Database** window

4. Select the **Macros** tab in the **Database** window

If necessary, move the **Database** window so that you can see the **Form Footer** area in your form. You must be able to see both the macro required in the **Database** window and the **Form Footer** area of your form on the screen.

5. Drag and drop the *Open Publisher details* macro from the **Macros** tab to the **Form Footer** area

6. Display the **Database** window again, and drag and drop the Print Preview *Books grouped on publisher* macro into the **Form Footer** area

On your Form Design, to resize the buttons to display the macro name:

7. Select the button

8. Open the **Format** menu

9. Choose **Size, To Fit**

Your final design should be similar to the illustration below.

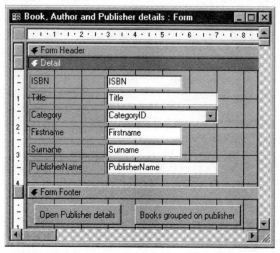

10. Save the changes to your form

11. Return to Form view

The control buttons are displayed in the footer area. To run the macro behind the button, simply click the button.

Try them out!

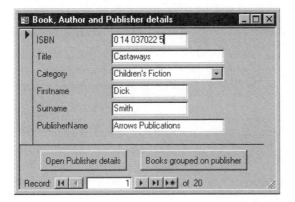

—— 12.6 A brief mention of modules ——

A module is a collection of Visual Basic, Applications Edition declarations, statements, and procedures that are stored together as a unit.

You can use modules to automate database tasks by using the power and flexibility of the Visual Basic programming language.

Using modules, you can:

● Create event-driven applications (a set of codes that runs when a particular event takes place – perhaps the click of a control button, or data entered into a field).

● Create your own modules (these would be listed on the **Modules** tab in the **Database** window).

or

● Use a custom procedure.

To exploit the facilities offered by the Access Modules object, you really need to be familiar with the Visual Basic programming language.

If you want to learn more about modules, browse the on-line help system. We can only make you aware of them in a Teach Yourself book – not teach you how to write them.

———— 12.7 Chapter summary ————

Macros and modules are extremely powerful objects. They can be utilised and exploited by database developers to automate the way in which Access works. An experienced database developer can use these objects to build very sophisticated databases that can be very easy to use.

In this chapter we have given you an introduction to macros and modules.

You have learnt how to:

● Create a macro.

● Run a macro.

● Assign a macro to a control button on a form.

APPENDIX

Category table data

CategoryID	Category Name
1	Adult Fiction
2	Animals
3	Astronomy
4	Children's Fiction
5	Computing
6	Cooking
7	Craft
8	Education
9	Family
10	Foreign Language
11	Gardening
12	Geography
13	Health
14	History
15	Music
16	Poetry
17	Religion
18	Romantic Fiction
19	Science
20	Travel

———— Author table data ————

AuthorID	Surname	Firstname	Date of Birth	Date of Death
1	Peterson	Brian		
2	McDonald	Alastair	12/01/36	
3	Jackson	Marion	24/06/55	
4	Adamson	Pauline		
5	Duncan	Wilma	04/07/38	
6	Ferguson	John	03/04/03	05/10/88
7	Jackson	Allan	10/12/40	02/10/93
8	Smith	Dick		
9	Schmit	Hans	12/12/52	
10	Camembert	Marion		
11	Meunier	Luc		
12	Allan	Isabelle	10/05/65	
13	Stephen	Moira		
14	MacDonald	Donald	12/12/20	01/03/78
15	Williams	Peter	10/10/30	
16	Borthwick	Anne		
17	Ferguson	Alan	04/12/45	
18	Wilson	Peter	12/01/30	
19	Smith	Ann		
20	Watson	George	22/10/45	

Nationality	Speciality	Notes
English	Romantic Fiction	Best seller "Hollywood Days"
Scottish	Poetry	
English	Travel	
Australian	Children's Fiction	
American	Travel	
Irish	Gardening	
Scottish	Travel	
Canadian	Children's Fiction	Best seller "The Mounty"
German	Computing	PC applications
French	Gardening	Best seller "Flowering Shrubs"
French	Cooking	
Scottish	Travel	
Scottish	Computing	PC applications
Scottish	Travel	
Irish	Science	School textbooks - mainly physics
Welsh	Astronomy	TV personality
English	Computing	Mainly Computer Science
Canadian	Children's Fiction	Famous for "Worst Wizard" books
American	Computing	PC applications
Austrian	Travel	Writer of TV books

—— Publisher table data ——

PublisherID	PublisherName	Address1	Address2	City
1	Hodder & Stoughton Ltd	338 Euston Road		LONDON
2	Borthwick-Henderson	Applewood House	Applewood Hill	OXFORD
3	Westward Lock Ltd	18 Clifftop Street		LONDON
4	Softcell Press	One Softcell Rise		ORLANDO
5	Christy Corporation	20 E 103rd Street		INDIANAPOLIS
6	Arrows Publications	Randall House	1 Cavalier Bridge Road	LONDON
7	Harry Cousin Ltd	10-23 Frosty Road	South Bank	LONDON
8	Beaver Books Ltd	7 Squirrel Lane		LONDON
9	Darling Kinghorn Ltd	2 Herbert Street		LONDON
10	City Publishing Company Ltd	7 Queen Street		EDINBURGH
11	Scrambler Publications Ltd	6-9 Prince Street		LONDON
12	BPU Publications	Europa House		Queen's Cross
13	Outreach College Press	Wilson Way West		LIVERPOOL
14	Carling & Sons plc	4 St Thomas' Park		LONDON
15	Trueform Press Ltd	Manderson House	8 George Street	LONDON

Postal Code	County	Country	Phone Number	Fax Number	E-mail Address
NW1 3BH		England	0171 738 6060	0171 738 9926	Hodst.co.uk
OX1 7DP	Oxfordshire	England	01865 333545	01865 333444	Bhend.co.uk
WIX 1RB		England	0171 333 4454	0171 222 4352	Westward.co.upk
33412-6641	Florida	USA			Softcell.pub.co
46290		USA			Christy.co
SW1V 2SA		England	0171 443 9000	0171 443 1000	JoeS@Arrows.co.uk
W6 8JB		England	0181 444 0808	0181 444 5000	Info@Harc.co.uk
W8 5TZ		England	0171 445 7000	0171 445 6000	
WC2E 8PS		England	0181 665 7766	0181 665 7000	Darkin.co.uk
EH1 3UG	Midlothian	Scotland	0131 445 6800	0131 445 6236	Scot@Citypub.co.uk
NW10AE		England	0181 556 4354	0181 556 3030	
	Herts	England			BPU.pub.co.uk
LP3		England			OCP.ac.uk
SW1					Carl.co.uk
SW3 6RB		England	0171 334 3344	0171 334 2000	

Book table data

ISBN	Title	AuthorID	PublisherID	CategoryID	Row Number
0 14 032382 3	In & Out Stories	8	11	4	3
0 14 037022 5	Castaways	8	6	4	12
0 14 930654 7	The 2nd World War	3	14	14	1
0 15 056473 6	Teach Yourself Access 7	13	1	5	12
0 345 12342 3	Campfire Cooking	20	8	6	21
0 34532 3751	Garden Shrubs	6	8	11	13
0 412 32132 2	African Drums	14	1	1	14
0 412 46512 1	Bits & Bytes	13	2	5	12
0 416 23765 3	West Highland Way	7	1	20	14
0 45 469861 2	Hamsters at Home	8	6	2	4
0 465 77654 3	Giant World Atlas	20	13	20	14
0 482 31456 1	Easy Internet	17	2	5	12
0 55345 456 2	The Night Sky	2	13	3	20
0 563 49124 5	Bread and Biscuits	11	7	6	21
0 576 26111 2	Crazy Comets	15	13	3	20
0 587 39561 0	Changing Skies	16	2	3	7
0 664 58123 4	Reading with the Under 5's	8	1	8	6
0 758 34512 1	Perfect Pizzas	11	15	6	21
0 85234 432 6	Outdoor Adventures	12	10	20	14
0 99988 452 1	The Tortoise in the Corner	4	6	4	12

Shelf Number	Number of copies	Publication year	Price	Reference	Lending	Picture
2	3	1987	£3.99	No	Yes	
2	2	1994	£4.50	No	Yes	
5	3	1988	£12.50	No	Yes	
3	2	1997	£7.99	No	Yes	
2	1	1995	£4.99	No	Yes	
2	2	1986	£4.99	No	Yes	
5	1	1992	£12.50	No	Yes	
3	2	1992	£9.99	No	Yes	
4	1	1992	£12.50	No	Yes	
2	1	1979	£4.50	No	Yes	
4	1	1991	£35.00	Yes	No	
2	2	1996	£9.99	No	Yes	
4	2	1991	£35.00	Yes	No	
3	2	1987	£12.50	No	Yes	
3	1	1989	£17.50	No	Yes	
5	2	1990	£10.99	No	Yes	
2	2	1991	£6.99	No	Yes	
5	2	1986	£9.99	No	Yes	
4	2	1985	£15.00	No	Yes	
3	2	1991	£6.50	No	Yes	

INDEX